START TO FINISH

MOTORBOATING

....

BARRY PICKTHALL

START TO FINISH

MOTORBOATING

·································

BARRY PICKTHALL

WILEY NAUTICAL

This edition first published 2010

© 2010 John Wiley & Sons Ltd

Registered office

John Wiley & Sons Ltd, The Atrium, Southern Gate, Chichester, West Sussex, PO19 8SQ, United Kingdom

For details of our global editorial offices, for customer services and for information about how to apply for permission to reuse the copyright material in this book please see our website at www.wiley.com.

Wiley also publishes its books in a variety of electronic formats. Some content that appears in print may not be available in electronic books.

Designations used by companies to distinguish their products are often claimed as trademarks. All brand names and product names used in this book are trade names, service marks, trademarks or registered trademarks of their respective owners. The publisher is not associated with any product or vendor mentioned in this book. This publication is designed to provide accurate and authoritative information in regard to the subject matter covered. It is sold on the understanding that the publisher is not engaged in rendering professional services. If professional advice or other expert assistance is required, the services of a competent professional should be sought.

This product has been derived in part from material obtained from the UK Hydrographic Office with the permission of the UK Hydrographic Office, Her Majesty's Stationery Office.

We would like to thank A&C Black for their kind permission to reproduce material from Andy du Port and Neville Featherstone's Reeds Almanac 2009, Adlard Coles Nautical, an imprint of A&C Black Publishers.

A catalogue record for this book is available from the British Library.

ISBN: 978-0-470-69751-1 (PB)

Designed and typeset in 8.5pt Frutiger LT Std by PPL Ltd
Illustrations by Greg Filip/PPL

Printed and bound by Toppan Leefung Printing Ltd, China

Contents

Getting started

I was first drawn to powerboating as a child through a passion for fishing. Rather than wait for the fish to come my way, I soon learned that it was far more profitable to chase after them. I rigged up a small outboard on the back of the family dinghy and spent endless hours trawling for mackerel or sitting anchored off the beach with worm-baited lines pulling up Dover sole.

From there it was a short enthusiastic jump first to waterskiing, then fast cruising from port to port. It is an adventurous, exciting, and fun sport that can appeal to all the family.

A fast seaworthy power cruiser can carry you a long way in a day: across the English Channel to taste the delights of French cuisine, run across the Gulf Stream from Miami or Fort Lauderdale to spend the day on a deserted beach in the Bahamas, or simply to get out to where the fish are running.

The latest electronic nav aids take the guess and stress out of navigation, and the ability to cruise at 20knots + becomes a major safety factor, giving you the ability to outrun bad weather.

Nowadays, many people discover the delights of getting afloat later in life, bypass the small fishing dinghy inauguration altogether and are introduced through friends or experiences on holiday, straight to high powered sports fishing or power cruisers.

That's fine, but buying a powerboat is often one of the biggest expenditures many of us will make, so it is prudent to know what you are doing before going afloat, or at least to have an experienced hand onboard to show you the ropes. Better still, enrol on an introductory sailing course like those organized by the UKSA to learn not just the rudiments of getting a boat to go where you want it to, but how to dock, communicate and navigate safely. These are all essential skills, and your choice of boat will be all the more informed once you are competent – and confident – enough, to take her out for the day or weekend.

This powerboat manual takes you through a step-by-step guide based on the UKSA's teaching programme and is designed to provide readers with a thorough grounding to enable you to manoeuvre, plan and make a passage safely.

Powerboating is a great recreation, not just for moving from A to B but opening opportunities to scuba diving, fishing, waterskiing and socialising. Whether your choice is an Orkney sports fishing boat, a Ribtec rigid bottom inflatable (RIB) or a power cruiser like the Tony Castro-designed Galleon 44 flybridge cruiser all featured in this book, everyone has the opportunity to enjoy being afloat.

You will love it!

Barry Pickthall

Powerboat types

What type of powerboat should I buy? The first-time buyer is confronted with bewildering choice of shapes and sizes, some of them very specialised and intended for varying conditions and uses. If your interest is fishing on rivers or lakes, then a small flat-bottomed boat that is light, stable and easy to transport could well be the boat for you.

Fishing offshore requires a more rugged design with greater freeboard and a hull shape that will slice through the seas rather than bounce uncomfortably over them.

Should cruising be your prime criteria, then size and number of berths may be your first consideration, but running costs and where to keep her should be a close second.

Hull shapes

Hull forms can be divided into two broad categories: displacement and planing.

Planing hulls obtain their dynamic lift from a combination of hull shape and the speed at which they move through the water. As speed increases, the hydrodynamic forces lift the hull up on top of the water, reducing drag and wave-making resistance to allow relatively high planing speeds. The transition point between displacement and planing is known as 'hump' speed'. This is where the hull generates enough 'lift' to rise up on top of the water and accelerates forward just as if a turbo has kicked in when driving a car.

Planing hull in slow displacement mode.

Same hull in full planing mode.

Displacement hulls

Traditional, non-planing types are known as displacement hulls. Working on Archimedes' principle that a floating object displaces its own weight of water at rest as well as at speed, these traditional hull shapes are continuing to push aside their own weight of water, setting up a wave at the bow and stern.

As speed increases, the height and distance between these two waves increases to the point where the hull is supported in the water by the wave generated by the bows, and the other at the stern, with a big dip in between.

At this point, the boat has reached its maximum displacement speed. This figure is in direct proportion to the length of the hull and can be calculated quite accurately using the equation:

$$\sqrt{\text{Waterline length} \times 1.4} = \text{hull speed}$$

Thus, a displacement hull with a waterline length of 25ft (7.62m) has an effective top speed of 7 knots.

If more power is applied, the hull will try to climb up its own bow wave, and the stern wave will fall back, leaving the transom to sink down in the trough, creating a great deal of wash and a wasteful consumption of fuel. Any further increase in speed can only be achieved by an inordinate and highly inefficient use of extra power.

Semi-displacement hulls

A semi-displacement hull is a hybrid of these two types, combining V-shaped forward sections that merge into flat or rounded profile aft. When pushed above displacement hull speed, this design type operates at the lower end planing mode speeds, providing a comfortable – though wet – ride through heavy seas. It is not as fuel efficient or as fast as a fully planing hull and invariably rolls more.

Wave pattern of a displacement hull operating above its design speed.

Wave pattern of a displacement hull operating at its design speed.

Nelson semi-displacement hull. Excellent sea boats, but very wet.

Elan 35 deep-V sports cruiser running at speed.

Planing hulls

The deep-V hull is the most popular form for fast offshore fishing and cruising powerboats. The sharp entry of the bow and V-shaped bottom, carried all the way back to the transom, minimises slamming and smoothes the boat's ride over waves. The widely flared bow adds to the forward buoyancy, limiting any tendency for the hull to bury its nose when running through following seas, and the addition of spray rails to knock down spray, also contribute to this 'lift'. At slow speed, the deep-V hull has more draft than a flat planing hull and behaves much more like a displacement design. The deeper the V or angle of deadrise, (often between 18° and 25°) the better the performance and ride in rough water. The trade-off is less speed in calmer conditions than flatter bottomed designs. Some designs incorporate a 'step' in the hull approximately 2/3rds of the way back from the bows. Also known as the 'vented' hull, the step is designed to suck air under the aft sections of the hull to lessen wetted area and resistance. The bubbles of air sucked in to the flow act like ball bearings to reduce friction.

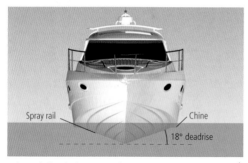

Spray rail
Chine
18° deadrise

A deep-V hull in displacement mode.

A deep-V hull in planing mode.

Orkney cathedral hulled unsinkable dory.

The vented Intrepid sports fishing hull. Air is sucked down through the step to lessen wetted area and resistance.

Cathedral hulls

The cathedral hull is a triple V-shaped planing monohull originally developed in America. It offers a wide rectangular full-length cockpit coupled with remarkable stability and load carrying capabilities. These open dories make excellent tenders and inshore rescue craft.

Catamarans

Powered catamarans are popular in Australia and parts of America, where they are used as fast fishing boats. These twin-hulled designs combine the good stability characteristics of the cathedral hull with the sea keeping qualities of a deep-V hull. Their performance is, however, more susceptible to weight than a deep-V hull.

Glacier Bay power catamaran.

Orkney Vanguard traditional sports/fishing boat

Orkney Boats have been building traditional go-anywhere sports fishing boats for more than 3 decades. The 19ft Vanguard used in illustrations throughout this book marries the traditions and strength of moulded clinker planking with the get-you-home-safely all-weather performance of pilot boat design thinking.

Built in Britain, the Orkney range of sports fishing boats can be found all over the world. Produced in sizes from 13–24ft (4–7.3m) the larger boats within the Orkney range have fully fitted cabins, while the smaller fishing boats can be purchased as open boats or with the addition of a fixed and folding cuddy.

Orkney Vanguard 190		
Length:	19.40ft	5.91m
Beam:	7.50ft	2.26m
Draft: (engine down):	2.50ft	0.76m
(engine tilted):	1.00ft	0.30m
Internal freeboard:	2.40ft	0.73m
Displacement:	2,359lb	1,070kg
Trailed weight:	3,240lb	1,470kg
Max engine:		100hp
Max speed:		30knots
Max payload:		6 persons or 1,323lb
Transport:		trailer
Design stability category:		C

Ribtec rigid bottom inflatable – RIB

The concept of marrying a deep-V hull to an inflatable collar around the gunwale was first developed by Atlantic College in Wales back in 1967. The idea was then carried forward by Royal National Lifeboat Institute (RNLI), which put a number of Atlantic 21 inshore lifeboats on station around the British Isles. The concept was then adopted by the military as rapid assault and rescue craft.

During the 1980s the good sea-keeping capabilities of the deep-V hull and inherent safety of the inflatable tubes which keep these boats buoyant even when full of water, has attracted a strong allegiance among the boating public worldwide. The Ribeye 6m RIB featured in this book is produced by Ribtec Ltd in the UK and is a fine example of the genre in terms of handling, performance, sea-keeping qualities and safety.

Rebtec Ribeye 6metre RIB		
Length:	19.68ft	6.00m
Beam:	7.48ft	2.28m
Draft: (engine down):	2.50ft	0.76m
(engine tilted):	1.54ft	0.47m
Tube diameter	1.50ft	0.46m
Air chambers:	5	1,070kg
Displacement:	1,962lb	890kg
Trailed weight:	2,844lb	1,290kg
Max engine:		120hp
Max speed:		40knots
Max payload:		8 persons or 2,425lb (1,100kg)
Transport:		trailer
Design stability category:		B

Galeon 440 Flybridge sports cruiser

The 44ft (13.42m) Galeon 440 Flybridge sports cruiser used in illustrations throughout this book is designed by Tony Castro and built in Poland. She is a particularly good example of the flybridge cruiser design with a large saloon, expansive owners' suite and two guest cabins. Stairs from the aft cabin lead up to the flybridge to provide a commanding position for the helmsman, and seating and sunbathing areas for guests. There is a second steering console at the forward end of the main saloon for when the weather is inclement. Powered by twin Volvo Penta diesel engines, she has a 400 mile range and cruising speed of 25knots.

Length:	44.03ft	13.42m
Beam:	13.45ft	4.10m
Draft:	3.94ft	1.20m
Displacement:	20.08tons	18,216kg
Max engine:		2 x 420/575KW/PS
Max speed:		33 knots
Crew limit:		12 persons
Design stability category:		B
Crew:		6 people

POLROS II

POL-5982

Edgewater 245 Centre console sports fishing boat

The 24ft 5in (7.4m) Edgewater 245 is typical of the deep V centre console sports fishing boats developed in America to carry you across the Gulf Stream to the fishing grounds and dive wrecks in the Bahamas or Catalina Islands off California.

These boats are extremely versatile. Their deep-V hulls cut through waves with ease while their high freeboard and wide midsections give added stability and the confidence to run at speed through beam and following seas. The designs have built-in fish and bait boxes, rod holders and stowage space, and larger models like this Edgewater 245 even have an enclosed toilet built into the central console.

Length:	24.50ft	7.40m
Beam:	8.50ft	2. 60m
Draft: (engine down):	2.50ft	0.76m
(engine tilted):	1.74ft	0.53m
Internal freeboard:	2.30ft	0.70m
Displacement:	3,400lb	1,543kg
Trailed weight:	3,240lb	1,470kg
Max engine:		350hp (single or twin outboards)
Max speed:		45 knots
Max payload:	11 persons or 3,700lb	1,680kg
Transport:		trailer
Design stability category:		B

Parts of the boat

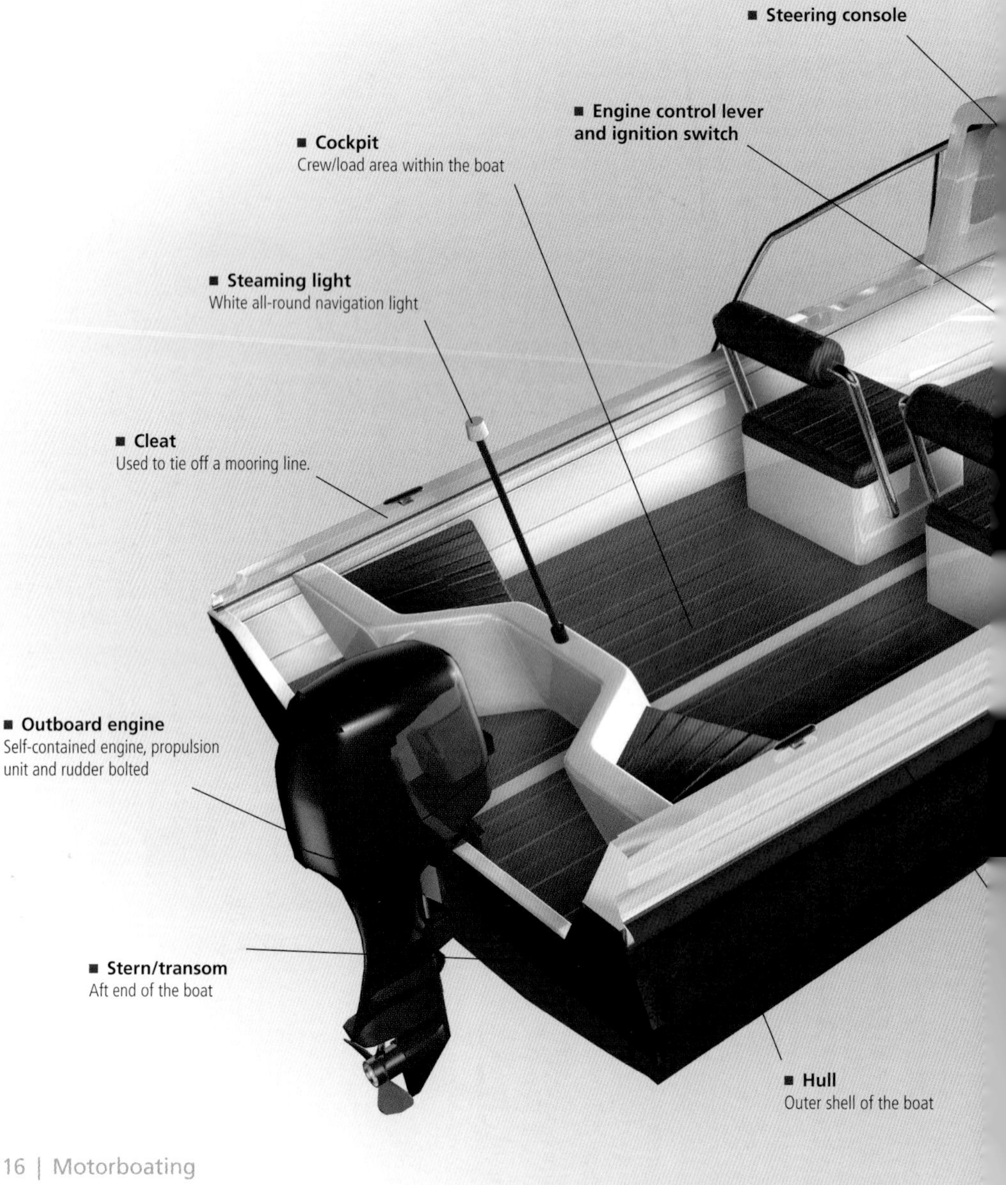

■ **Steering console**

■ **Engine control lever and ignition switch**

■ **Cockpit**
Crew/load area within the boat

■ **Steaming light**
White all-round navigation light

■ **Cleat**
Used to tie off a mooring line.

■ **Outboard engine**
Self-contained engine, propulsion unit and rudder bolted

■ **Stern/transom**
Aft end of the boat

■ **Hull**
Outer shell of the boat

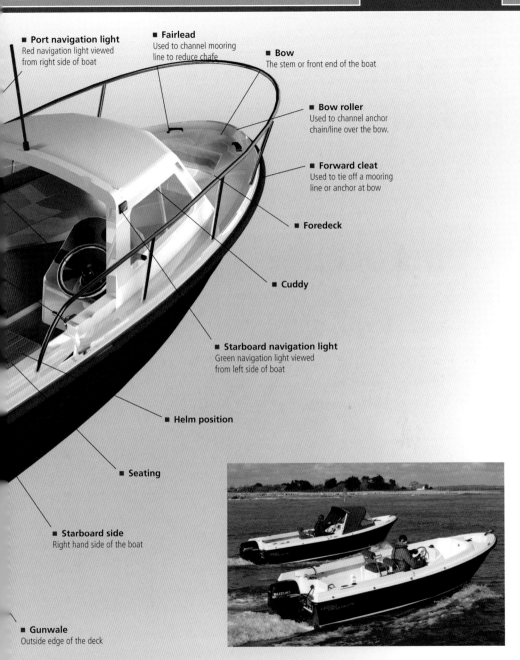

■ **Port navigation light**
Red navigation light viewed from right side of boat

■ **Fairlead**
Used to channel mooring line to reduce chafe

■ **Bow**
The stem or front end of the boat

■ **Bow roller**
Used to channel anchor chain/line over the bow.

■ **Forward cleat**
Used to tie off a mooring line or anchor at bow

■ **Foredeck**

■ **Cuddy**

■ **Starboard navigation light**
Green navigation light viewed from left side of boat

■ **Helm position**

■ **Seating**

■ **Starboard side**
Right hand side of the boat

■ **Gunwale**
Outside edge of the deck

3D Rigid inflatable boat (RIB)

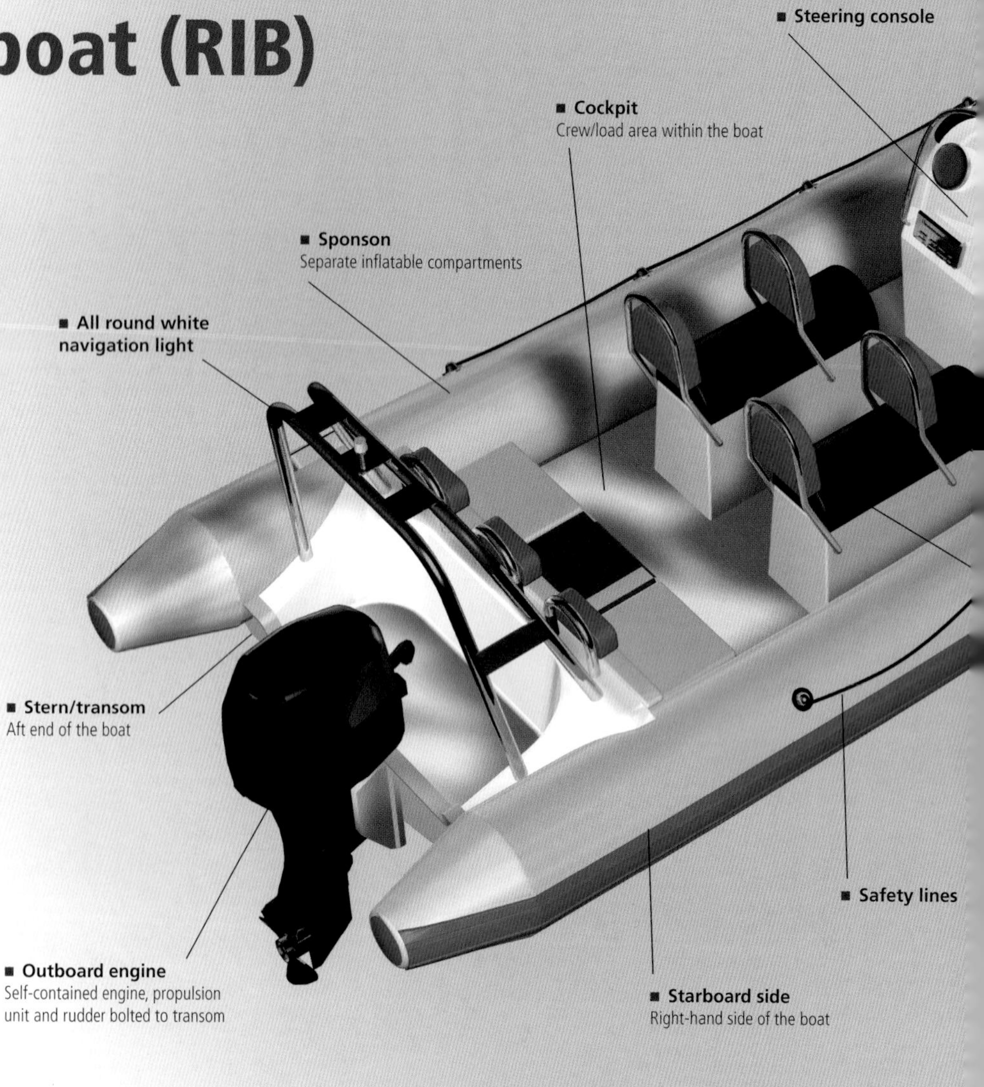

■ Steering console

■ Cockpit
Crew/load area within the boat

■ Sponson
Separate inflatable compartments

■ All round white navigation light

■ Stern/transom
Aft end of the boat

■ Safety lines

■ Outboard engine
Self-contained engine, propulsion
unit and rudder bolted to transom

■ Starboard side
Right-hand side of the boat

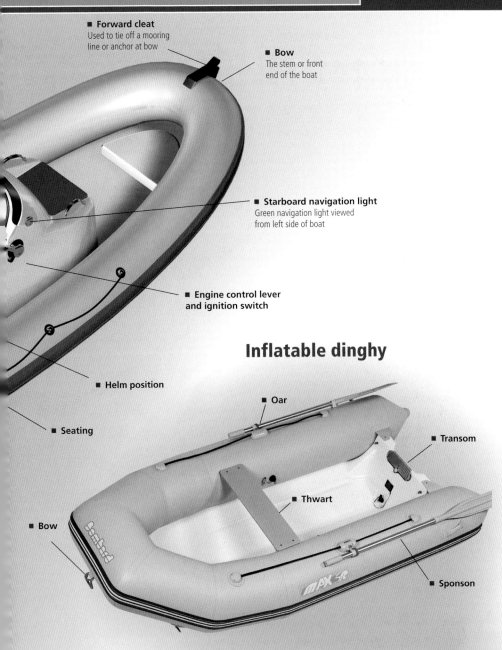

Forward cleat
Used to tie off a mooring
line or anchor at bow

Bow
The stem or front
end of the boat

Starboard navigation light
Green navigation light viewed
from left side of boat

**Engine control lever
and ignition switch**

Helm position

Seating

Inflatable dinghy

Oar

Transom

Thwart

Bow

Sponson

Galeon 440 Flybridge cruiser

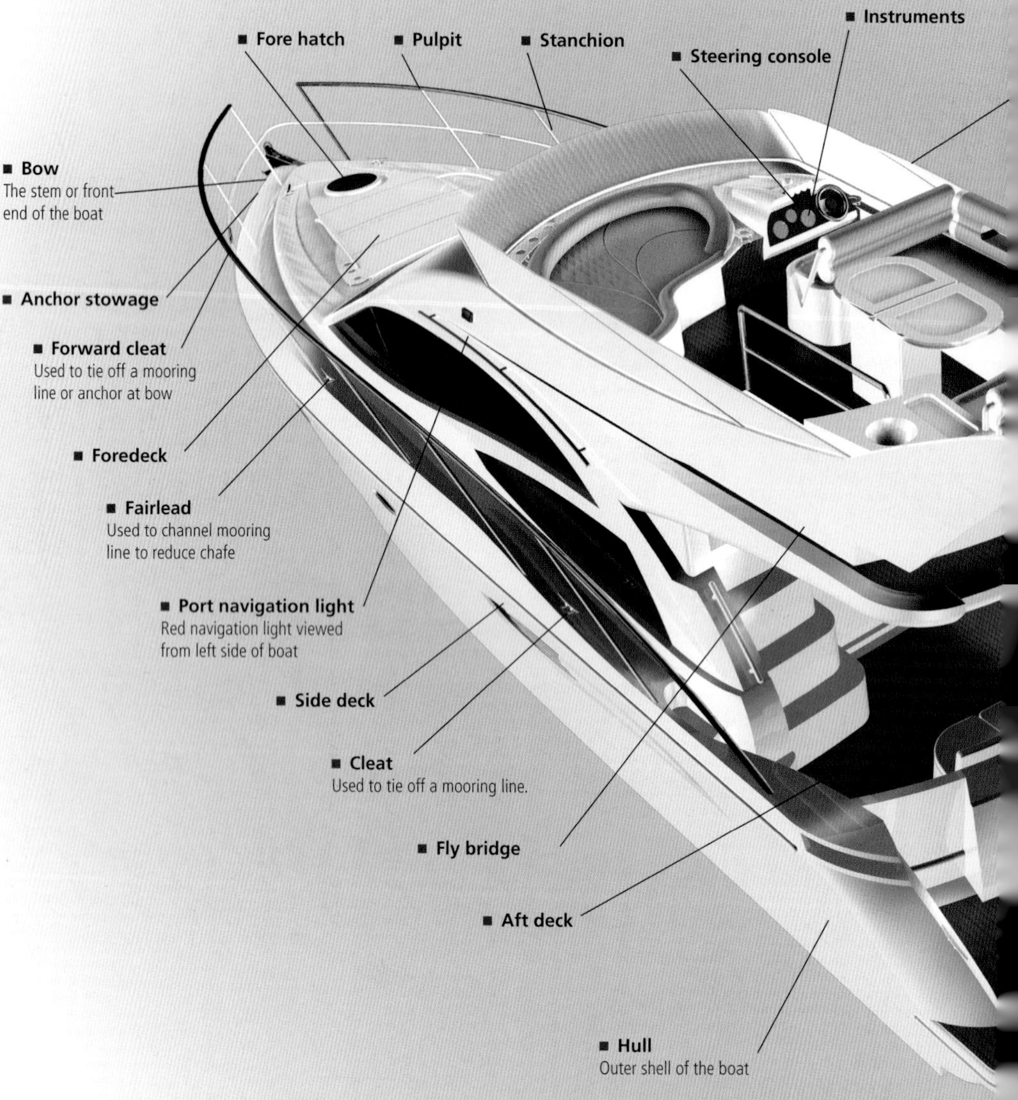

■ **Fore hatch**　■ **Pulpit**　■ **Stanchion**

■ **Instruments**

■ **Steering console**

■ **Bow**
The stem or front
end of the boat

■ **Anchor stowage**

■ **Forward cleat**
Used to tie off a mooring
line or anchor at bow

■ **Foredeck**

■ **Fairlead**
Used to channel mooring
line to reduce chafe

■ **Port navigation light**
Red navigation light viewed
from left side of boat

■ **Side deck**

■ **Cleat**
Used to tie off a mooring line.

■ **Fly bridge**

■ **Aft deck**

■ **Hull**
Outer shell of the boat

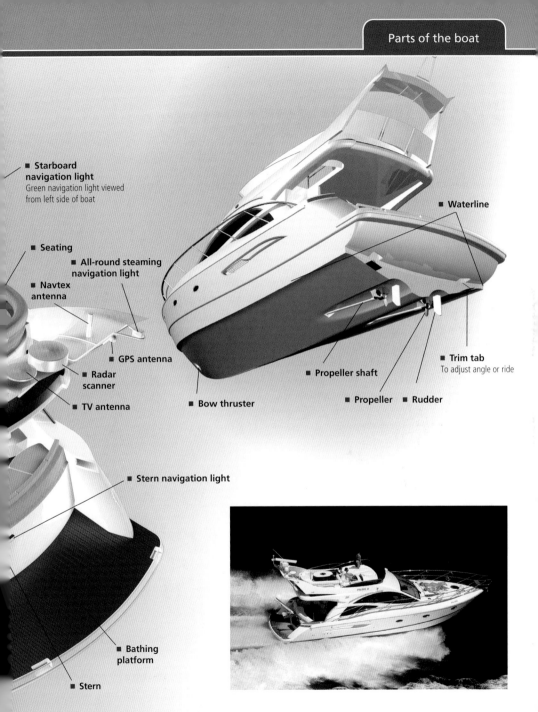

- **Starboard navigation light**
Green navigation light viewed from left side of boat

- **Waterline**

- **Seating**

- **All-round steaming navigation light**

- **Navtex antenna**

- **GPS antenna**

- **Radar scanner**

- **TV antenna**

- **Bow thruster**

- **Propeller shaft**

- **Trim tab**
To adjust angle or ride

- **Propeller** - **Rudder**

- **Stern navigation light**

- **Bathing platform**

- **Stern**

Propulsion systems

There are four types of propulsion – the outboard engine, the inboard engine, the inboard/outdrive and the waterjet. All these propulsion systems rely on the screw propeller to provide the thrust.

The propeller has radiating blades that form part of a helical or spiral surface and operates like an auger cutting a hole through wood. A propeller's thrust is proportional to the mass of water it is acting on. Large-bladed propellers with less pitch are more efficient than smaller props with a deeper pitch. On small pleasure boats, limited draft and constraints of clearance from the hull conspire to limit prop diameter to something smaller than optimal size. Their performance depends on the area and pitch of the blades. This is measured by the theoretical amount the propeller will move forward with each complete turn. Thus, a 251/4-inch (33cm) pitch propeller will move that distance with each revolution.

In practice, propellers perform well below their theoretical pitch figure because no account is made for the weight of the hull and the resistance the boat generates in the water. The figures are distorted even more by the speed at which the propeller turns.

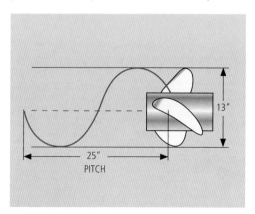

Pitch is the theoretical distance that the propeller will travel on one rotation.

In practice propellers perform well below their pitch figure because of cavitation and slippage.

The faster the spin, the greater the cavitation, or bubbles that form on the blade tips when the prop is under load. Cavitation is caused when the pressure on one part of the blade falls below ambient pressure (atmospheric + hydrostatic head), and a vacuum is formed. This is often experienced during fast acceleration and sharp cornering. The telltale signs are a sudden increase in revs and a reduction in speed.

Propellers have improved considerably over the years, and most engine manufacturers offer an advice service to match propeller type and pitch with the type and use of your boat Three-bladed propellers provide a greater top speed at the expense of low end accelerations. Four-bladed designs have better low-end power but at the expense of top-end speed. Volvo Penta's Duoprop and IPS forward facing dual prop outdrive legs have two contra-rotating props which increase efficiency by as much as 15% and eliminate prop walk.

Lightweight electric outboard.

Standard propellers supplied with outboard and outdrives are invariably aluminium. These are easily damaged, and since any chinks on the trailing edge of the blades can have a marked effect on performance, these are often replaced with more durable stainless steel propellers.

Composite props provide a cheaper alternative and some designs have the provision to replace individual blades if they are damaged.

Bronze propellers are often used on inboard powered boats kept afloat because of their greater resistance to corrosion. Zinc sacrificial anodes must be fitted on the shaft and hull to overcome electrolysis problems associated with saltwater applications.

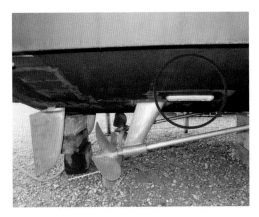

Zinc sacrificial plate fitted close to shaft and bronze prop, rudder and P-bracket save them from electolytic action.

Outboards

The outboard motor is the most common form of propulsion for smaller boats, offering compact weatherproof units from 1.5hp to more than 300hp. At one end of the market are the light, simple, battery powered electric auxiliaries used to power a tender or provide super-quiet manoeuvrability when fishing. At the other end are the compact 2–3 litre race-bred models with sophisticated electronic engine management systems. In between is an enormous choice of engines, including two and four-stroke, powering props or waterjet systems.

Two and four-stroke systems have very different characteristics. The two-stroke has a better power-to-weight ratio and superior low-down torque than a four-stroke, making them a better choice for waterskiing and other applications where fast acceleration is required. On the downside, they use more fuel than a four-stroke and produce greater emissions.

The four-stroke really scores with more torque at the top end of the rev range, coupled with quieter, smoother running without the smoky exhaust that remains a trademark of all two-strokes.

Inboards

Most marine inboard engines are adapted car and truck motors. Inboard installations offer the ability of placing the engines where their weight has the least effect and are connected via a reduction gearbox directly to the prop shaft. However, the exposed shafts, struts and P-brackets all contribute to parasitic drag. The greater the incline of the shaft, the less efficient forward thrust becomes. The shaft rotation in the water generates a surprising amount of friction and can also lead to considerable vibration.

Twin inboard engine installation with props and rudders.

Inboard/outdrives

The problems of drag and vibrations associated with inboard installations are largely overcome by the inboard/outboard configuration, where an inboard engine drives a steerable outdrive leg that can be raised like an outboard when navigating in shallow waters and allow the boat to take to the ground.

Their advantages are simple installation, and low noise and vibration levels. Their disadvantage is that engine weight is centred well aft, which can cause some boats to hobbyhorse badly when heading into rough seas. Volvo's IPS forward facing drive system overcomes this by fitting the outdrive leg through the bottom of the boat, rather than the transom which has the effect of moving the weight forward.

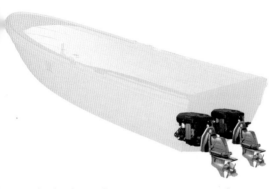

Twin inboard/outdrive installation.

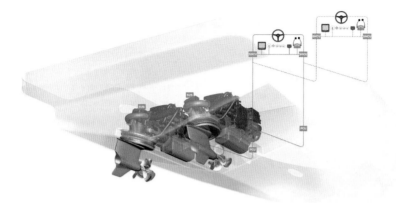

Twin Volvo IPS forward facing inboard/outdrives.

Waterjets

Waterjet units follow Newton's Third Law of Motion in which every action has an equal and opposite reaction. Just like the backward thrust that is felt when holding a powerful fire hose, the discharge of a high-velocity stream of water from the jet unit generates a reaction force in the opposite direction, which is transferred through to the boat to propel it forward.

The one-piece jet unit is mounted inboard at the back of the boat with the nozzle extending through the transom. The water intake fits flush within a flat section in the bottom of the hull. As the water enters, the flow is accelerated by an impeller through a reducing diameter tube to be discharged at high velocity through the nozzle. Steerage is achieved by turning the outer nozzle to port or starboard to deflect the water one side or the other, and reverse is achieved by a 'bucket' that hinges down over the nozzle to deflect the jet stream back under the boat. These controls are remarkably efficient, and in an emergency, the boat can be stopped within its own length when the bucket is deployed and full thrust maintained.

Waterjets operate at the high end of the power spectrum more efficiently than prop driven boats, but are more susceptible to weed and flotsam gumming up the works in badly weeded or polluted waters.

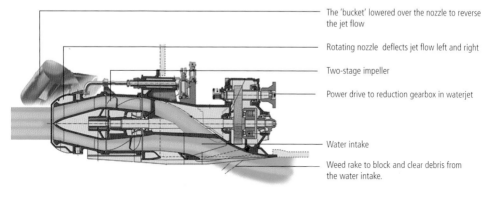

The 'bucket' lowered over the nozzle to reverse the jet flow

Rotating nozzle deflects jet flow left and right

Two-stage impeller

Power drive to reduction gearbox in waterjet

Water intake

Weed rake to block and clear debris from the water intake.

Cutaway of a Castoldi waterjet propulsion unit.

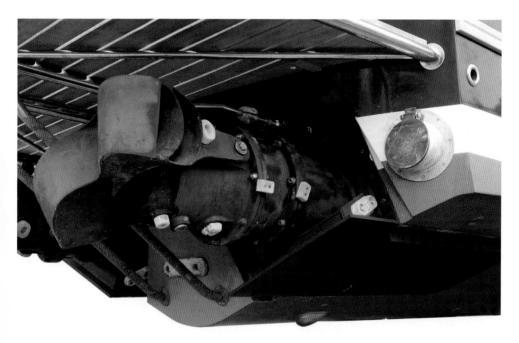

Photo of twin Castoldi waterjet propulsion units with the intake and 'bucket 'positioned over the outlet to reverse the jet flow in clear view.

Buying a powerboat

It could be one of the most expensive purchases you make, so deposits and payments should be protected just as if you were buying a property.

If you are buying through a dealer or from stock, ensure that the company operates a client account and make payments payable directly to that account.

Check that the contract contains a full specification or inventory. If stage payments are used to purchase hull mouldings, engines and equipment, ensure that titles for these items are transferred to you, clearly identified to the hull number, and insured.

If buying second-hand, check to see whether the vessel is subject to a mortgage. If it is, this will be listed on the boat's registration documents and recorded in the Small Ships Register.

Make a search, just as you would with the title documents for a property. If the boat is subject to a marine mortgage or loan, ensure that this is discharged before completing the purchase.

Title documentation should include:

- Part I Registration
- Builder's Certificate
- Previous Bills of Sale
- Evidence of RCD compliance
- Evidence of VAT status (in the EU)

Ensure that the contract is subject to a sea trial and survey. When buying second-hand, commission an independent survey. Don't rely on one provided by the owner.

Transporting and launching trailable powerboats

Sports fishing boats like the Orkney are designed to be dry sailed: stored ashore on their trailers during the week so that they don't attract weed or require antifouling, and launched and recovered on their trailer each time they are used. Many marinas now have a secure pen to store the boats and some operate dry stack storage using forklift trucks to store, launch and recover them on demand. But if you have the space to store the boat on its trailer at home, then it is often simpler and certainly cheaper to launch and recover the boat yourself.

Towing regulations in many countries stipulate that the dry weight of the towing vehicle must, at a minimum, equal the weight of the trailer, which should also have brakes. Some countries also restrict the driving age to those over 21 who must also pass an additional test, so do check that your driving licence allows you to tow a heavy trailer and your vehicle is compatible before setting out on the road.

The Orkney weighs 3,240lb (1,470kg) and with her outboard engine raised, draws only 12in (30cm) of water so can be towed behind any mid-range family car.

Trailing abroad

Regulations vary between countries, so check with the tourist authorities of the states you intend to drive through to ensure that your boat and trailer complies with local laws. As crew, many countries now require that the skipper holds a valid VHF certificate and

International Certificate of Competence (ICC) or higher qualification. It is best to check with the national boating authority in each country, and carry the certificates with you.

Planning

The difference between a safe, simple launch and a dangerous or stressful one is down to planning and preparation.

Check out your intended launch site ahead of time by calling the harbour master, river authority or marina office. Will there be enough water? Are there facilities to park the car and trailer? How steep is the slipway? Front and rear wheel drive vehicles will struggle on steep inclines especially if the surface is slippery. Some public slipways are free, but many are not. Local bylaws sometimes restrict the type of boat that can be launched and a permit may be required.

What time is high water? This may dictate launch and recovery times.

Standard requirements

The vehicle

- Car and trailer insurance documents with international travel endorsements
- Registration documents
- Warning triangle and set of spare bulbs.

The boat

- Original VAT sales receipt
- Insurance certificate with international travel endorsements
- Purchase flares at your destination. Flares are banned on most ferries, and some countries require a firearms certificate.

Checklist for launching

- Remove side straps, covers and lighting board
- Keep winch strap attached to bow
- Insert bungs, and close drainage flaps and inspection hatches
- Allow 30 minutes for wheel bearings to cool down before immersion
- Check engine oil and fuel levels.

❶ Ensure the trailer is loaded slightly front heavy to avoid it 'snaking' out of control when braking. Plug in trailer lights and check that they are all working. Loop the safety wire around the ball hitch and lock the jockey wheel in place.

❷ Tie the boat down on its trailer using adjustable webbing straps or a lorry driver's hitch. Check that outboard/outdrives are locked in the raised position, and fit a day-glow warning/protective bag over the propellers.

❸ Modern multi-roller trailers make launching and recovery of even quite large boats easy for one person to do, without the need to immerse the trailer.

❹ The multi-rollers at the back of the trailer pivot and swivel automatically to take the same attitude as the boat as it rolls off into the water.

5 Take care not to immerse the brakes and hubs, especially in sea water. If there is no alternative, then allow 30 minutes for them to cool down before immersion and rinse with fresh water straight after.

6 Control the boat as it slides down the trailer by lacing the painter around the trailer handles and keep the winch wire attached to the boat. If the boat does run away, keep well clear of the winch handle.

7 Keep a wary eye open for passing vessels kicking up a wash. This can affect the smooth operation of launching, so wait for the water to flatten before starting.

8 Once afloat, lead the boat away from the trailer to avoid waves banging the hull up against it. Recover the trailer and park above the high-water mark.

Recovery

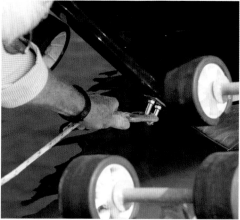

❶ Trim the engine/sterndrive up to stop it from grounding, and drive the boat onto the trailer.

❷ Attach the winch line to the bow and tension it to keep the boat pressed against the rollers.

❸ Line the boat up with the centre of the trailer and take account of wind and stream.

❹ Winch the boat up onto the trailer.

5 Check that the boat remains central on the trailer and that the supporting rollers do not capsize.

6 Once on the trailer, check that the rollers are firmly against the hull and adjust if necessary.

7 Flush the engine cooling system with fresh water to rinse out the salt water within the cooling system.

8 Wash down the boat and trailer. The latest trailers are fitted with hose connection points to flush the brakes.

Knots, ropes and running rigging

The best way to learn knots is to carry a piece of thin cord in your pocket and practise during quiet moments until you can do them with your eyes shut.

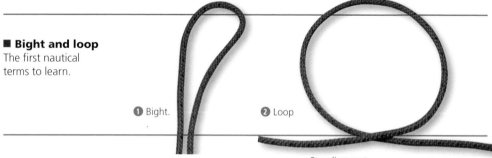

■ Bight and loop
The first nautical terms to learn.

❶ Bight.

❷ Loop

Standing part

■ Reef knot
Used to tie two lines of equal thickness together, such as reefing lines and sail ties. Remember the rule: left over right. Right over left.

❶ Bring the two ends of the rope together, cross left over right and tuck under.

❷ Continuing with the same end, cross right over left and tuck under.

❸ Pull tight and check.

For an interactive lesson, go to **www.uksa.org/ knotmaster** and master 5 knots in 5 days.

■ Tugman's hitch
Used to attach a towline to a strong point such as a sampson post, cleat or winch. This knot holds well and is easy to undo even under load. Also known as the Lighterman's and Boatman's hitch.

❶ Take several turns arour the post, cleat or winch.

■ Bowline

Ties a nonslip knot in the end of a rope. Used to form a secure loop in the end of a mooring line or to tie a sheet to the clew of a sail. Remember the adage: *The rabbit comes out of its hole, runs round the tree then goes back down the hole again.*

1 Form a crossing turn in the end of the rope.

2 Form the loop (rabbit hole) to the size required, with the outer end upward.

3 Round the back of the standing part.

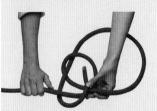

4 And guide it down through the small loop.

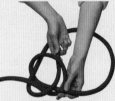

5 Pull the end through the small loop.

6 Pull tight and check the tail is long enough not to pull out.

2 Take the working end under the standing part and over the post.

3 Repeat 2 but in the opposite direction.

4 Repeat 2 again to lock off.

■ Cleating a rope

The OXO method of tying off a mooring line or halyard on a horn cleat.

❶ Take a full turn around the cleat.   ❷ Cross over in a figure-of-eight....   ❸ ...and finish with a final turn around the cleat.

■ Single sheet bend
Used to tie two lines of unequal thickness together, such as sail ties.

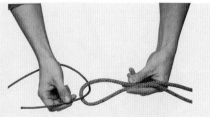 

❶ Form a bight in the thicker rope.   ❷ Pass the end of the thinner rope up through the bight and under.

■ Coiling rope

Loose rope ends like halyard tails should be coiled and secured with the tail so that they are ready to be shaken out at a moment's notice.

1 Take the end of the rope in one hand, stretch it out with the other, twist it clockwise...

2 ...and transfer each loop to the first hand.

3 Once coiled, make several turns with the working end around the coils and feed through the top loop...

4 ...and pull tight.

3 Repeat 2 but in the opposite direction.

4 Repeat 2 again to lock off.

■ Lorry Driver's hitch

Used to tension a line or strap securing a boat on its trailer or on deck. Very easy to undo. Tie off one end of the rope to a secure point and throw over the boat, then pass the working end of the rope through a secure point on the opposite side.

❶ Form a loop in the rope at the top of the downward side.

❷ Now pull a short length of the standing end of the rope back through the loop to form two further loops above and below.

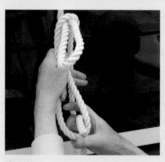

❸ Pass the working end through the lower loop...

❹ ...and tension down.

❺ Secure with two half hitches.

❻ For added security tie the upper loop into a half hitch around the standing part.

■ Clove hitch
Used to attach a temporary line to a rail or ring.

1 Easy to undo, so make sure you leave a long working end.

2 Pass the working end around the object and back across itself.

3 Form another half hitch.

4 Pull through...

5 ...And tighten.

■ Round turn and two half hitches
Used to attach a line to a post or ring. Easy to untie, even under load, so ideal for securing a mooring line or fenders.

1 Pass the end round the back and form a half hitch.

2 Repeat to form a second half hitch.

3 Pull tight.

What to wear

Wearing the right clothing to keep you warm and dry is the first requisite to maximising enjoyment afloat. There is a wide variety of specialist clothing available for the fashion conscious, but almost any waterproof jacket will keep the spray off. Protect yourself from the sun by slipping on a long sleeved tee-shirt, slapping on a hat and slopping on plenty of high factor sun cream. In wetter, colder climes, take account of the wind chill factor – the speed of the boat can lower the ambient temperature by several degrees, so wrap up well and wear waterproof trousers as well as a top if you think you might get wet.

Children get cold much quicker than adults. Ensure that they keep warm and dry and plan your trips accordingly.

The other priority is a lifejacket that will keep you afloat with your head above water in the event of a dunking. Self-inflating lifejackets are not suitable for use in open boats because they inflate whenever they get wet, and not just when you fall overboard. They do, however, provide an additional safety measure on larger powerboats.

Buoyancy aids are available to match all shapes and sizes. They are even available for pets. Make sure that your choice is type-approved by your national standards authority, sized to match your body weight and fits comfortably over your oilskins.

Buoyancy aids sold in the European Union are CE tested and approved. Buoyancy aids are usually '50 Newton class' flotation aids (CE code 393), providing a minimum of 50N (11lb/15.5kg) of buoyant force. Some buoyancy aids classed as '100N' have the force to flip a swimmer over onto their back, include a neck support and are usually worn by children or inexperienced swimmers.

In the USA, choose a buoyancy aid that is type-approved by the United States Coast Guard. Type II buoyancy aids are recommended for confident swimmers. Type III flotation aids have 69N (15.5lb/17kg) of buoyant force and include a collar to keep the face of an unconscious person out of the water.

What to wear offshore

Sailing offshore requires rather more protection than taking a spin around a lake

or harbour, and the better the clothing, the more you will enjoy it. When you are on an overnight passage or longer, clothing has to keep you warm and dry in the cold of night as well as daytime.

Staying warm and keeping dry are really two sides of the same coin as far as thermal insulation is concerned. Cotton underclothes for instance can absorb up to 100% of their own weight in water or sweat, and with this moisture next to the skin, body heat is sapped out 30 times faster than with a dry fabric. By contrast, hollow-fibred, polyester thermal undergarments have the unique ability to wick perspiration away from the skin by capillary action into the outer garments, thus keeping the skin warm and dry. The decks can get very wet and slippery, so good boots with nonslip soles are another priority.

Personal protection
- Wear enough clothes to keep warm
- Always have sufficient protection from the sun, and wear good quality sunglasses
- Always wear footwear with closed toes when outside the cockpit. There are many trip hazards on the deck and it is all too easy to injure yourself.
- Wear a lifejacket and encourage others to do the same.

Safety gear
The golden rule on any vessel is to 'keep one hand for the yacht… and one for yourself'. The latest self-inflating lifejackets, with all-important crotch straps, will keep you afloat with your head above water indefinitely, but it is far better to avoid falling overboard in the first place.

Left: A self-inflating lifejacket with safety harness and quick-release carbine hook. *Right:* A buoyancy vest.

Lifejackets

The best lifejackets are those that incorporate a safety harness with a 6ft (2m) line and self-locking quick-release carbine hooks at each end for you to attach to jack stays or tether points around the cockpit, flybridge and deck

It is a good rule to insist that crew members always wear their lifejacket whenever they don their oilskins when they come out of the cabin. A good rule is when not to wear a lifejacket, rather than when to wear it.

The lifejacket should have a minimum buoyancy of 150 Newtons, and should be tested when first purchased by being inflated orally and left for a period, and then annually.

Keep spare gas canisters onboard. The skipper must ensure that the crew has been issued with lifejackets / harnesses and instructed on their use before going to sea. Whilst at sea, the crew shall wear lifejackets:

- when the skipper requests
- on deck at night
- in fog
- if the individual wants to
- if the individual is a non-swimmer

Use of lifelines

A lifeline attached to a jackstay or safety point will keep you connected to the boat in the event of you falling overboard.

Other personal safety equipment to be kept ready to hand in the pockets of your oilskins are:

- knife or multi-purpose tool
- LED flashlight
- whistle
- personal man-overboard beacon (MOB) if the vessel is equipped with a MOB receiver
- orange smoke flare.

A quick release safety line attached to a strong point on the boat.

Kill cord safety line between helmsman and console.

Crew briefing showing safety equipment and rules onboard.

Kill cord

The kill cord is an engine cut-out device that slides in behind a spring-loaded button on the engine control of most open powerboats. The other end is attached around the helmsman's leg or lifejacket and will cut the engine should he or she fall overboard.

The engine will not start unless the kill cord is in place.

Always carry a spare kill cord in the boat so that the engine can be re-started and driven back to pick the person up.

Safety briefing

Before casting off, give the crew a safety briefing.

- Wearing and use of lifejackets
- Flares and first-aid locations
- VHF radio – how to send a MAY DAY
- Engine controls and use of kill cord
- Basic boat handling
- Anchoring
- Show them where you plan to go on the chart to familiarise them with their surroundings
- Explain the dos and don'ts onboard
- No riding on the bow when the boat is in motion – if they fall overboard they will finish up as mincemeat in the props!
- On large power cruisers, no one goes forward to the bow without the OK of the helmsman
- Beware of climbing up to the flybridge when the boat is in motion
- Use of the marine toilet – a dark art to most novices!

Essential equipment & safety briefing

After checking your protective clothing and lifejacket, the open powerboat should have a safety check before setting off.

Safety equipment
- **Anchor and line.** A folding Danforth anchor takes up least space. Together with the anchor line, which can double as a towing warp, pack at least 5ft (1.5m) of chain to act as ground tackle. These must be stowed securely.
- **The anchor line/tow rope** should be at least three times the length of the speedboat and with a minimum breaking strain of twice the weight of the boat and crew.
- **Bailer, bucket and sponge.** Attach retaining lanyards to the bucket and bailer to stop them from floating away. If you are going out for the day, carry spare clothing and personal items.
- **Waterproof bag.** To carry first-aid kit, flares (2 hand-held red, 2 parachute, 1 orange smoke), VHF radio or mobile phone, charts, water, energy drinks and bars.
- **Compass.** GPS set and water-proofed chart showing local area with channel marks and hazards.
- **Tool roll:** Spark plugs, spanners, allen keys, screw drivers and water dispersant oil.
- **Spare fuel.** Two spare fuel filters.

Offshore safety equipment checklist

- **Distress flares**
2 orange smoke hand flares
4 red parachute rockets
6 red hand flares
2 lifebuoys
- **Emergency Position Indicating Radio Beacon (EPIRB)** if doing significant offshore passages
- **Search & Rescue Transponder (SART)** if doing significant offshore sailing
- **2 buckets** with lanyards attached to handles
- **2 bilge pumps** (manual and electric) – the manual one should operate from the cockpit
- **Radar reflector** (an active radar transponder provides best visibility to other vessels)
- **Fog horn** + spare canisters
- **Spare fuel, oil and water** (10ltrs of each + funnel)
- **Liferaft** (serviced annually)
- **Boat hook**
- **Fenders**
- **Spare lines**
- **Compass**
- **GPS**
- **Courtesy + Q flags**
- **Protective clothing.** (Lifejacket or harness for each crew member (including spare gas bottles for the lifejackets and 2 spare lifelines). Each lifejacket should have a built-in harness, a crotch strap, a whistle, and light)
- **Grab bag** (carrying food, water, flares, etc)
- **Anchor and chain + kedge and line**

First-aid kit + manual

The longer the passage, the better stocked the first aid box should be. When cruising inshore, a simple domestic first aid kit, will suffice, when stored in a waterproof container. If you are planning a weekend or week-long voyage, more comprehensive emergency medical supplies are required.

Onboard safety checklist

▪ Tool kit

- Adjustable wrench
- Cable ties
- Centre punch
- Electrical crimping tool + connectors
- Electrical tape
- Emery cloth or boards
- Epoxy rapid cement
- Gasket cement
- Hammer
- Hand drill
- Hose clips
- Junior hacksaw
- Long nose pliers
- Mole grips
- Plastic piping
- Punch
- Round file
- Rubber mallet
- Set of allen keys
- Set of drill bits
- Set of flat head screwdrivers
- Set of Phillips screwdrivers
- Set of spanners
- Socket set
- Stanley knife
- Spare batteries
- Spare bulbs and fuses for nav lights and torches
- Tape measure
- Vernier callipers
- Waterproof grease
- Wire brush

▪ Galley

- Fire blanket
- Safety strop
- Fire extinguishers in each cabin and remote controlled extinguisher in engine compartment
- Fire blanket within easy reach of galley
- Powerful searchlight

▪ Nav station

- Admiralty list of lights
- Admiralty radio signals
- Almanac
- Back-up radio receiver (wind up)
- Barometer
- Binoculars
- Boat data file
- Breton plotter
- Calculator
- Current charts for region
- Dividers
- Echo sounder
- Emergency torch (wind up)
- Eraser
- GPS
- Log book
- Hand-bearing compass
- Mobile phone + charger
- Pencils and sharpener
- Pilot books + tidal atlas
- Portable VHF + charger + emergency aerial
- Symbols and abbreviations chart

Engine checks

Your engine is the beating heart of your boat. If it stops, so do you, so check over the unit each time before you go out. The sea is a harsh environment and salt water is particularly corrosive.

Best practice

- Keep fuel tanks topped up to limit condensation contaminating the fuel
- Inspect the engine with a torch before and after a passage for oil and water leaks
- Keep the engine clean and use oil-absorbing pads in the bilges to contain drips
- Check rubber pipes for signs of perishing or splits
- Monitor sacrificial anodes protecting engine, shafts, propeller and rudder from electrolysis and replace when necessary
- Follow manufacturer's recommendations for servicing.
- Check hydraulic oil levels. Top up as necessary.

Daily checks

- Oil levels in engine and gearbox. Top up as necessary.
- Colour of oil. If the oil has changed, track down the cause and repair. If cream or grey, then water is present. Drain oil, replace filters and fill with fresh oil.
- Check fresh water coolant levels, top up as necessary.
- Belt tension and wear. Check steering. Adjust or replace as necessary alternator and water pump belts
- Check fuel levels. Top up as necessary.

- Check fuel filters for water and particles. Strip and clean as necessary
- Check seawater inlet and strainer for debris. Clear as necessary and remember to re-open stop-cock before starting engine.

Engine spares to carry onboard

- 2 x spare alternator belt
- 2 x spare engine oil filters
- 2 x spare fuel filters
- 2 x spare water pump filter
- Spare water pump belt
- 2 x spare water pump impeller

Console checks

- Check throttles are in neutral and set for start-up.
- Turbo-charged diesel engines set on tick-over
- Normally aspirated diesel and petrol engines set at half revs
- Turn batteries ON
- Pre-heat diesel engine
- Start engine
- Outboard petrol engines normally require some choke (unless already warm) and throttle set to start
- Once engine has started, reduce revs to tick-over and close choke. Do not rev until engine has warmed up.
- Check cooling water is discharging
- Keep an engine log to record running hours, temperature and consumption figures. This will help fault-finding and troubleshooting later.
- Mark normal operating levels on oil pressure, volts and water temperature gauges to provide quick alerts to any abnormalities.

Steering console

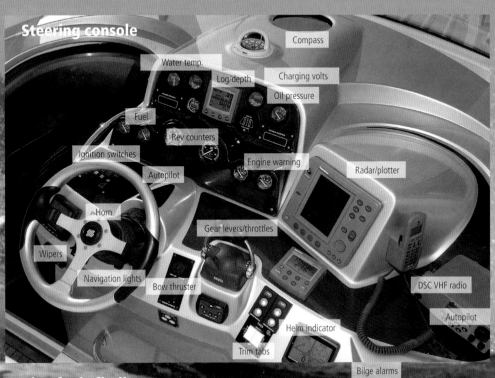

Compass
Water temp.
Log/depth
Charging volts
Oil pressure
Fuel
Rev counters
Ignition switches
Engine warning
Autopilot
Radar/plotter
Horn
Gear levers/throttles
Wipers
Navigation lights
Bow thruster
DSC VHF radio
Autopilot
Helm indicator
Trim tabs
Bilge alarms

Engine fault-finding

Engine fails to turn over when ignition is activated	Check throttle controls are in neutral. Check battery and leads. Check circuit breakers and battery switches are ON.
Outboard engine fails to fire	Spray engine and electrics with WD40 or similar moisture displacing fluid.
Diesel engine falters	Almost certainly fuel starvation. Check fuel levels. Check fuel filter for water or contamination and replace if necessary then bleed engine.
Air in the fuel system	Stop engines if safe to do so. Check fuel line from tank to engine for leaks, then bleed engine.
Overheating	1. Check for blockage at inlet or in strainer. 2. Lack of water in heat exchanger or expansion tank. 3. Leak in waterway pipework. Check for cooling water in engine bay. 4. Broken or worn impeller in waterpump.
2-stroke outboard will not start	Spark plugs oiled up. Remove and clean, then turn engine over to get rid of excess fuel in the cylinders before screwing plugs back. Re-start with less choke and more throttle.

Getting onboard from dinghy and dock

Dinghies

Tenders are just as their name describes – tippy. Always wear a buoyancy aid or lifejacket before getting in one, and always step into the centre of the dinghy, never on the side. Let the rower position themselves amidships first before loading the bow and stern.

Never overload the dinghy. Make two trips if necessary, the first with people, and the second to carry the stores.

Always shine a light at night to alert other vessels to your position and carry a small anchor and line.

Offshore motor cruisers

Modern motor cruisers invariably have a boarding/bathing platform at the stern, which makes it easier to get on and off the boat.

Secure the dinghy side-on to the stern using bow and stern lines, and always step out from the centre of the dinghy, and never the gunwale.

When there is a swell running, the gunwale of the dinghy can become trapped under the transom, so moor the dinghy alongside and not at the stern.

Boarding vessels without a bathing platform or transom step is made easier by using removable steps or fender step that hang down over the gunwale.

Never pull yourself up on the lifelines or stanchion posts because your weight can loosen the fastenings and lead to leaks. When stepping aboard from the dock, use the bathing platform at the stern. If there is no platform, step across the gunwale into the aft cockpit gate.

If the vessel has lifelines running around the gunwale, climb on board through the 'gate' by opening the pelican hooks, and steady yourself with your hands on the reinforced stanchions. Replace the gate lines and secure the pelican hooks once on board.

Rules of the road

All vessels, from the smallest rowing tender to the largest supertanker, are governed by the same rules, known as the International Regulations for Preventing Collisions at Sea or IRPCS. The IRPCS are published in many forms, and for the price of a beer you can pick up a pocket-sized copy at any nautical bookstore – this is strongly recommended for any skipper. The IRPCS cover all aspects and scenarios of vessel interaction at sea. These are summarised by Rule 2, which makes law the application of good seamanship above the blind following of the later Rules – in other words to avoid immediate danger, a departure from the Rules may be necessary.

Rule 3 defines vessel types and nautical terms. In particular, a power driven vessel is defined as one propelled by machinery, including a yacht motor-sailing.

Rule 5 dictates that a proper lookout should be kept at all times by sight and hearing, as well as by all other means appropriate, e.g. using radar correctly in restricted visibility.

One of the most common ways for a vessel to get in trouble is to be going too fast for the circumstances. All the factors that affect a boat's safe speed are detailed in Rule 6. These come down to common sense and the awareness of where you are and what is around you. Very importantly it mentions the limitations of radar equipment – just because a vessel is fitted with radar there is no guarantee that it is working properly or that the operator knows what he or she is doing! Radar assisted collisions are caused by the incorrect use of radar information – if you don't know how to interpret it, don't assume it will magically keep you safe in restricted visibility.

The assessment of whether a risk of collision exists or not is discussed in Rule 7. This also mentions the dangers of scanty radar information! If an approaching vessel is on a reasonably constant bearing, then there is such a risk – this bearing can be checked using a compass, or by lining the approaching vessel up with a stanchion, for example. In confined waters with large vessels, make sure that you look at the entire length of the other vessel – on occasions, if the bow doesn't get you the stern will.

Rule 8 outlines action to avoid collision. The fundamentals are that this action should be early, easily visible to the other vessel and with due regard to the observance of good seamanship. You can change either or both of your speed and heading, and if you're doing so at night make sure you show the other vessel a different aspect light. Importantly, if you happen to be the stand-on vessel, you need to watch the oncoming vessel carefully and if necessary take avoiding action yourself if you cannot see any change. This is also emphasised in Rule 16.

Rule 9 governs what to do if you meet a large vessel in a narrow channel or harbour, and requires vessels of less than 65.6ft (20m) in length and sailing vessels not to impede the passage of a vessel which can safely navigate only within such a narrow channel. Think about your actions early in relation to the wind direction, tide or current flow and other vessels in your area. Options may include timing your entrance to the harbour so as to miss the shipping, sailing alongside, picking up a mooring till the traffic has passed, sailing into shallow water or out of the main channel, or even just turning around and sailing away from the danger. One classic mistake is to get too close to the bow of an oncoming vessel, forcing them out into the channel and trapping you between them and the side of the harbour. Remember that not all power boaters are aware of the mechanics of tacking upwind and don't understand why you are zigzagging in front of them.

Harbour authorities may have local bylaws which supersede the IRPCS inside their jurisdiction, such as allowing fishing boats to trawl in the harbour, banning the use of spinnakers, or giving commercial shipping absolute rights over all types of pleasure craft.

Such special rules should conform as closely as possible to the IPRCS and it is important to get the relevant information from the harbour office or harbour master's staff before setting out.

Rule 10 covers Traffic Separation Schemes, essentially highways for shipping in open waters. They control the movement of vessels in congested areas by regulating opposing flows.

Traffic Separation Schemes are divided into three areas:

- Inshore Traffic Zones on either side of the two highways can be used by vessels less than 65.6ft (20m) or sailing vessels. They are also frequently used by fishing vessels when fishing. Large vessels may also use an inshore traffic zone when en route to a port or to avoid immediate danger.
- Traffic Lanes are normally 3 miles (5km) wide or more. These lanes are usually used only by larger vessels. If you enter one of these lanes, do so at a shallow angle to filter in with the flow of traffic and do not impede the safe passage of any shipping.
- The Separation Zone is the central reservation dividing the two traffic lanes (the 'purple patch' on Admiralty charts). Small vessels may only use the separation lanes when crossing the area.

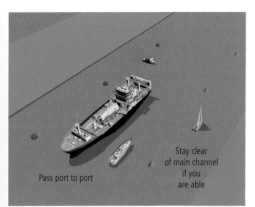

Pass port to port

Stay clear
of main channel
if you
are able

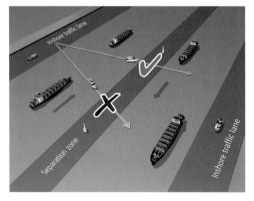

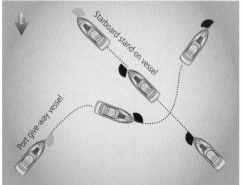

Rules of the road for vessels less than 65.6ft (20m) are as follows:

- Whenever possible stay away from the Traffic Lanes; use the Inshore Traffic Zone
- You shall not impede vessels using the Traffic Lanes
- If you have to cross the lanes then do so with your heading at right angles to the traffic flow

An overtaking vessel must keep clear of the slower vessel until they are past and clear. Rule 13 defines you to be overtaking if you are coming up on another vessel from an angle more than 22.5° abaft her beam. In other words, if you are approaching her and can only see her stern light. It doesn't matter whether you are a sailing yacht overtaking a powerboat – as the overtaking vessel you must stay clear.

An obvious collision situation is the Head on Situation. Rule 14 applies when you are under power, and you should alter course to starboard to avoid the collision. Remember, if both vessels are sailing this doesn't apply. Here, the sailing rules given in Rule 12 govern your actions.

When a Crossing Situation under power occurs, Rule 15 tells us that the vessel which has the other on her starboard side is the give-way vessel, and should take avoiding action to avoid crossing ahead of the other vessel, generally by altering course to starboard and passing behind her. A good way of remembering this is to think of the navigation light that you would

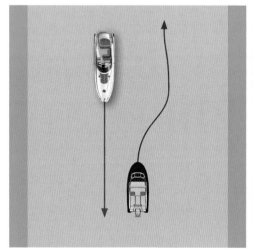

Pass port to port and keep to the correct side of the channel.

see – green means go, red means stop.

All these rules have spoken about the actions of the give-way vessel. The stand-on vessel also has responsibilities, detailed in Rule 17, to keep your course and speed, but be ready to take avoiding action if necessary.

Rule 18 defines the pecking order of who should give way to whom. Sailing vessels are generally required to keep out of the way of vessels not under command, restricted in their ability to manoeuvre, or engaged in fishing. See the list of vessels on page 58 that sailing boats must give way to and the shapes or flags that tell us why.

Navigation in Restricted Visibility is a much misunderstood rule. Rule 19 covers this, and it is vital to understand that the rules describing vessel interaction (Rules 12 – 18) do not apply when the visibility is such that the vessels are not in sight of each other. It boils down to a few important points:

- Proceed at a safe speed so you can manoeuvre easily
- If you detect another vessel by radar alone and you determine that a risk of collision exists, then take avoiding action as early as possible. There is no set option, but avoid turning to port for a vessel forward of the beam, and avoid a course alteration towards a vessel on or abaft the beam. Often the easiest option is to slow right down early on, or stop if you are not sure of the situation.
- Without radar: if you hear a vessel forward of the beam, then slow right down while still keeping steerage, and be extremely cautious until the risk has passed.

Shipping

Keep a watchful eye open for ships. Their speed can be very deceptive. Even in restricted waters, these vessels can be making as much as 15 knots in order to keep steerage way during turns. That means they will be bearing down on you at the rate of 1 mile every 4 minutes, so a ship that was on the horizon one minute can be a real hazard within 10–15 minutes.

Ships may also be constrained to the deep-water channel and unable to alter course to avoid you. Remember that visibility from the ship's bridge is very restricted. A small yacht will often 'disappear' from the view of the pilot and helm when more than half a mile ahead, so don't even consider crossing ahead unless you are absolutely sure you can get across in time. When crossing a channel, sail well within your personal limits. Large vessels will generate a temporary wind shadow, so

Fog can limit visibility to just a few metres. Proceed with extreme caution.

be aware and prepared should you lose sail power when the ship passes by. Commercial ships are busy earning a living. Sailors, on the other hand, are out there for enjoyment, so be considerate, keep well out of the way and abide by the rules.

Fishing/Trawling	⧓
Restricted in ability to manoeuvre Both of the above will be moving slowly.	⦙
Constrained by Draught The big boats will stay inside the buoyed channel.	▮
Not under Command Rare near the coast.	⦂
Underwater Operations Dredging or pipe laying. Probably stationary or moving very slowly.	
Diving. Dive boats fly flag **Alpha**. Keep well clear to avoid divers 'popping up' in front of you.	
Work boats can fly the flags **Romeo Yankee** which mean: 'Pass me slowly – no wash'.	

Sound signals

Powerboats are fond of making sound signals as it is easy for them – they just press a button. Sailors in open keelboats normally don't have the signalling equipment necessary to draw attention to themselves, and can only communicate their intentions by using bold manoeuvres in good time. The sound signals you are most likely to hear will be short (•) or long (–) blasts. Long tends to be more than 4 seconds.

•	I am turning to starboard.
••	I am turning to port.
•••	I am slowing down or going backwards.
•••••	I am unclear of your intentions (and getting worried).
–	I am coming (possibly round a corner or under a bridge).

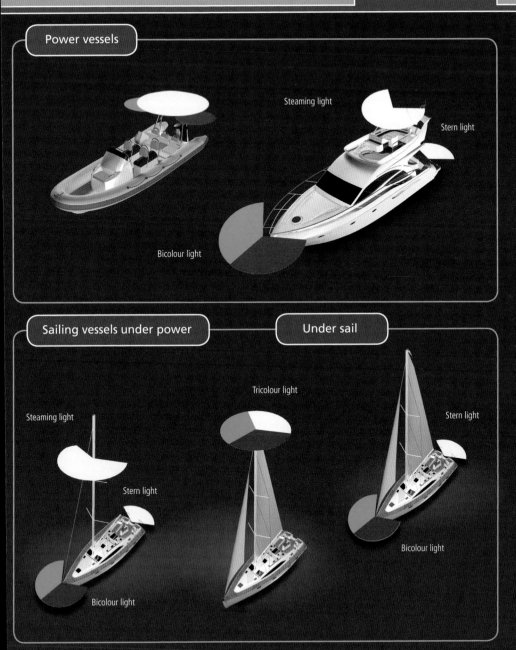

Power vessels

Steaming light

Stern light

Bicolour light

Sailing vessels under power

Under sail

Steaming light

Stern light

Bicolour light

Tricolour light

Stern light

Bicolour light

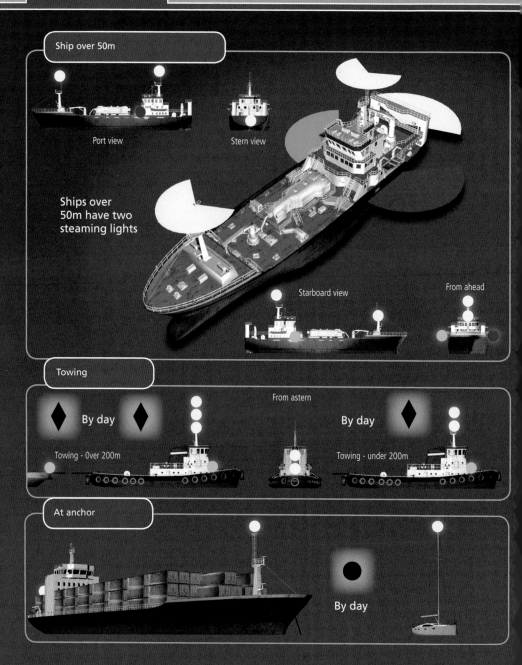

Ship over 50m

Port view

Stern view

Ships over 50m have two steaming lights

Starboard view

From ahead

Towing

From astern

By day

By day

Towing - Over 200m

Towing - under 200m

At anchor

By day

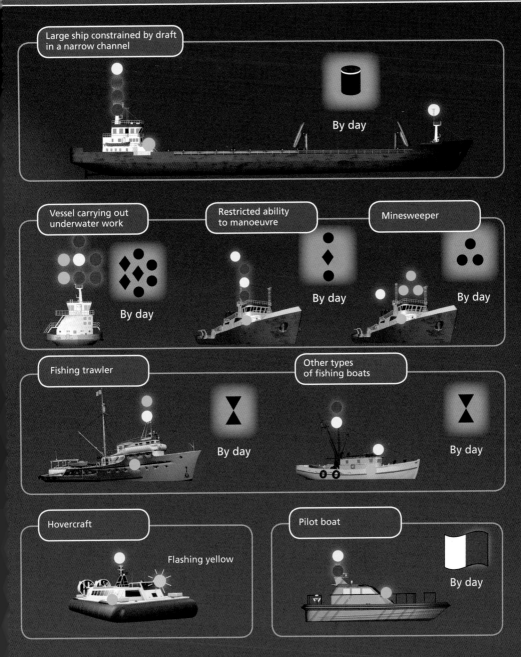

Large ship constrained by draft in a narrow channel

By day

Vessel carrying out underwater work

By day

Restricted ability to manoeuvre

By day

Minesweeper

By day

Fishing trawler

By day

Other types of fishing boats

By day

Hovercraft

Flashing yellow

Pilot boat

By day

Boat handling and trim – mooring and anchoring

Handling any sized powerboat needs practice, preferably in a wide open space, to find out how she behaves going astern, the effect windage has on the hull and, most importantly, the distance she needs to stop. Entering a narrow marina berth is no time to start learning her foibles. The key to successful manoeuvring is to do everything in slow motion without fuss, and approach at a controlled speed.

As Steve Rouse, the UKSA's chief powerboat instructor, is quick to tell his students whenever they use the throttles heavy-handedly, 'That could be expensive!' Anything more than a light-handed click on the gear lever from neutral to forward or reverse when manoeuvring in close quarters will propel the boat hard into another vessel or the dock.

Pivot points

When moving forward, a powerboat pivots around a point just forward of the centreline. When moving astern, this pivot point moves near to the stern because the propellers are pulling the boat round. This change of turning point can be put to good effect when handling at low speed in a confined area.

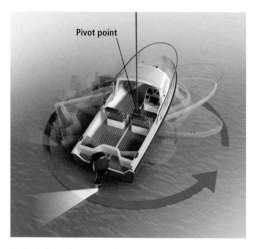

Moving in forward gear, a powerboat pivots around a point just forward of the centreline.

In reverse, this pivot point moves aft. As a result, the boat is much more responsive when turning.

Prop walk/wash

Thrust from the propeller also has a substantial 'paddle wheel' effect on boat handling, and once you know which way it is going to push the stern, this too can be harnessed to work for you when manoeuvring.

When putting the engine in gear, the propeller tends to pull the stern sideways in the same direction as its rotation. This is termed 'prop walk'. Thus a clockwise rotating prop will walk the stern to starboard when starting out in forward gear, and to port when engaged in reverse. Test what the natural inclination is for your powerboat and plan your entry and exit from the dock to maximise these traits rather than fight them.

The wash over the rudder from a quick burst of thrust from the propeller can also have a dramatic effect in spinning the boat round with little forward motion. By giving

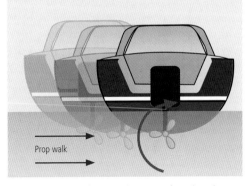

Prop walk

The clockwise rotation of the prop when put into forward gear has an initial effect of 'walking' the stern of the boat to the right.

a series of 'power bursts' fore and aft while holding the helm hard over, the boat can be turned round in a confined area, sometimes within its own length.

When forward gear is engaged, the flow of water from the propeller immediately

In forward gear, the clockwise turning propeller 'walks' the stern to the right (starboard).

In reverse gear, the propeller is turning anti-clockwise and 'walks' the stern to the left (port).

hits the rudder. This can be used to provide a turning force before the boat is moving at all. With the rudder angled hard over, the prop wash is deflected to one side and pushes the stern round in the opposite direction. Going astern can be another matter though, since the rudder needs 3–4 knots of water flow across it before it becomes effective.

Prop walk and wash is most significant with inboard, single shaft and separate rudder installations. With twin-prop installations, the propellers are engineered to counter-rotate to negate the effect of prop walk.

Outboard and inboard/outdrives do not produce prop wash (unless they have an additional rudder added behind the propeller as seen on some inland waterways boats) because the drive leg, which acts as the rudder, is ahead of the propeller. In these cases, a bow thruster makes the whole business of manoeuvring so much easier, providing a second pivot point close to the bow to spin the boat round.

With twin engine installations, the propellers counter-rotate to balance each other, whlch negates the effect of prop walk. Twin engined boats can be turned round in their own length by putting the outer engine forward and engaging the inner engine in reverse.

The bow thruster (a stern thruster is also available) is your 'get out of goal free' card when it comes to tight manoeuvring. The transverse drive will give the hull a sideways push into or away from the dock and help to turn the bow. They are operated by a joystick sited close the the wheel.

Turning

1–2 Short burst forward. Prop wash on rudder pushes bows round to starboard.

2–3 Short burst astern with rudder held over on port, pulls bows further round to starboard.

3–4 Repeat burst forward, completes 180° turn.

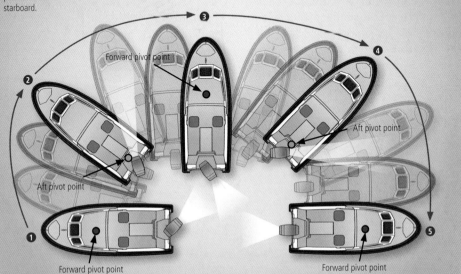

Forward pivot point

Aft pivot point

Aft pivot point

Forward pivot point

Forward pivot point

By maximising prop wash over the rudder and the effect of prop walk in pushing the stern round, it is possible to turn a vessel in little more than its own length by alternating between forward and reverse gears. This is how it is done:

❶ Turn the engine/rudder hard to starboard and keep it there. Engage forward gear and give the throttle a short burst. Thrust from the prop will be deflected to starboard by the rudder to push the stern round to port.

❷ Engage reverse for a short burst to stop the boat, put rudder on opposite lock and prop walk will pull the stern further to port.

❸ Engage forward gear and repeat 1.

❹ Engage reverse and repeat 2.

❺ As the vessel is lined up on new course, centre the rudder, engage forward gear and motor away.

If there is a strong wind blowing, bear that in mind and use the wind to aid the turn.

Tip

Turn the wheel first, then engage gear to maximise prop wash and thrust.

Turning – twin shaft, outboard or outdrives

Twin-screw configurations are the easiest to manoeuvre because the outer engine has greater leverage. Turning to starboard, you can either engage the port (outside) engine in forward and leave the starboard (inside) engine in idle to make a sharp left hand turn …

…Or put the port engine into reverse and the boat will spin round in its own length.

- Water flow on a buoy
- Weed or flotsam flowing down-stream

The bows of planing powerboats in particular have little grip in the water and are easily blown round by the wind. The boat's natural tendency is to lie side on to the wind, so keeping the bow's head to wind in strong conditions is not easy, even with a bow thruster.

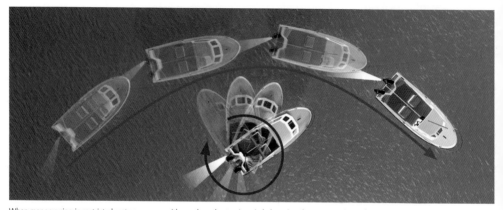

When manoeuvring in restricted waters, you can either reduce the turning circle by using the outer engine only, or put one engine in forward and the other in reverse to turn the boat in its own length.

Outside elements

Strong winds or tidal stream will have a considerable effect on a powerboat when manoeuvring. The golden rule is to always turn towards the strongest element.

The tidal stream is like a conveyor belt, moving the boat along in one direction. When coming alongside, always head upstream. This makes the boat slower over the ground and retains steerageway and control. To assess the direction of tidal stream, look for:

- Bubbles or eddies flowing past a moored vessel or pier

The best solution is to sit stern-to to the wind and use reverse thrust to hold your position. Reversing moves the pivot point aft, providing much greater control.

To assess the wind direction, look for:

- Flags flying around the marina or dock
- Direction of wind wavelets on the water
- Wind indicators on mastheads.

Tip

Use wind and stream to assist any manoeuvre. Do not work against them.

Trim

The correct running trim not only makes the boat's motion more comfortable, it saves fuel too. The first consideration is to concentrate moveable items in the centre of the boat and not shove them away in the bows or stern lockers. Extra weight in the ends only accentuates the sickening hobbyhorse effect in a seaway.

With planing hulls, the prime objective is to get the boat up on the plane quickly, then running level over the water. If the boat has a stern-down attitude, it may struggle to get on the plane. If it is bow-down, then it will be heavy to steer – and very wet!

Trim adjustors

Outboards and outdrive legs have electric or hydraulic rams to adjust their running angle up or down from a rocker switch sited either on the dashboard or back of the control box

- Trim the power leg down forces the bow down and will reduce slamming when running into head seas.
- Trim the power leg up will lift the bow and reduce the chance of burying the front of the boat when running down a following sea.
- Many planing powerboats are also equipped with adjustable trim tabs mounted on either side of the transom to fine-tune the boat's running angle.

These tabs can also level the boat laterally when running through beam seas or when the effect of the wind lifts one side of the hull. Pushing one tab down will raise that side of the boat back onto a more even keel.

Trim the outboard/outdrive down has the effect of pushing the bow down and reduce slamming in head seas.

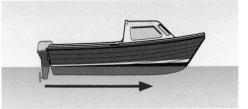
Outboard/outdrive trimmed level for flat water conditions.

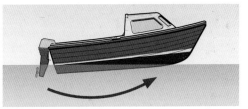
Outboard/outdrive trimmed up pushes the bow up to reduce the chance of it burying in when running in following seas.

Typical outdrive and trim tab installation.

Keeping a powerboat trimmed right requires constant adjustment. Tabs or power trim down may help to get the boat on the plane faster.

Trimmed correctly, the helm will be lighter without pull to either side and engine revs may rise slightly.

Tip

Tab down when running into head sea. Tab up when running into a follow sea. Experiment to see what suits your boat best.

Fenders

These are used to protect the boat when moored alongside a pontoon, harbour wall or another vessel.

Deploy them early when preparing the fore and aft mooring lines. At least three should be concentrated down the side and a larger 'ball' fender should be deployed near the bow.

Tie the fender lines with a round turn and two half hitches to the handrail and set them high enough to protrude above the pontoon.

Adjust fenders to protect hull from rubbing against the pontoon.

Have one large roving fender ready to deploy in the event of miscalculation.

When mooring alongside a harbour wall, use a fender board (plank) outboard of the fenders to level out the uneven surface.

Once the boat is completely secured, the fenders should be adjusted so that they are all doing a particular job. Usually they are hung at the same height for aesthetic reasons, but if you are expecting some swell then it may be a good idea to have some hung high and some hung lower than normal in case the boat rolls at the berth.

General notes on mooring

Ideally, each mooring line should be a separate one, and secured to a separate strong point on both the boat and the pontoon. This ensures that if there is a breakage for some reason the boat will still be secured by the other lines.

When approaching a berth, the ideal is to be able to stop the powerboat in a controlled manner in the correct position so that your

Have roving fenders at the ready.

crewmembers can tie the boat to whatever you are aiming for. The two major factors affecting your ability to stop are wind and tide. It is important to know, both by calculation and observation, what effect they are having on the boat in relation to your berth and to use these combined forces to slow you down.

The tide will ALWAYS move the boat bodily, and the wind will ALWAYS blow the bow away from it. Make a judgement on which has the stronger effect by checking the flow around a buoy or pier, and look at the effect the wind is having on vessels tied to swinging moorings, and make your approach into the stream or wind.

If the weather conditions are not kind, there is nothing wrong with asking the marina for help – by having a person on the pontoon to take lines or, if conditions are really bad, by coming out in a tender to act as a thruster. It is much better to get help and berth safely than not to ask and pile into someone else's pride and joy.

Whenever you are leaving a berth you have three main objectives:

- not to injure your crew or damage your boat
- not to damage any other vessels or facilities
- to leave harbour with everyone on board

Here's a mental checklist to go through:

- Look at the tidal flow flowing past the powerboat since there may be a local eddy that is different to the overall tidal movement. This tidal flow will bodily move the boat.
- Look at the wind direction and strength – this will blow the bows one way or another
- Ask yourself what would happen to the boat if all your mooring lines were released at the same time and decide which ones are important. For example, if you are moored port side alongside a pontoon, with a one-knot tide coming from bow to stern and a force 3 blowing from 45° on your starboard bow and you suddenly lost all of your lines, then your boat would be pushed back along the pontoon by the wind. Using this information, you need a line to stop you moving backwards – your stern spring – and a line to control your bow – your bow line. The other two lines are immaterial, and can be removed.

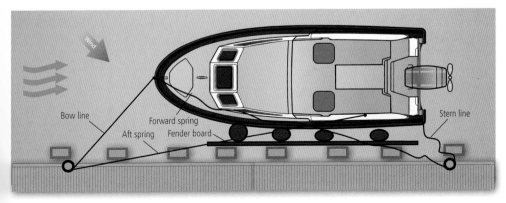

Bow line
Forward spring
Aft spring Fender board
Stern line
Wind

Reversing out on a bow spring

- As Steve Rouse, the UKSA's chief powerboat instructor, is keen to impress on his students, 'the back end of the boat is the expensive end – protect it!'
- Powerboats have the power to overcome the effects of tidal stream and wind. By reversing out, you have far more control. Move away forward, and the likelihood is the square stern will kick in and damage the transom, bathing platform or outdrives against the wall or pontoon – expensive!
- To leave, rig a large fender to protect the bows and run a spring from the bow to a bollard amidships.
  - Turn the wheel in and motor forward to pivot the stern away from the pontoon
  - Engage neutral gear
  - Bowman slips the bow spring
  - Engage reverse until the boat is in clear water.
- There is nothing wrong with having a crew member on the pontoon to release lines from an awkward spot, and picking him up from an outer pontoon or vessel later – you will still have the correct number when you leave the harbour!
- Most problems encountered when leaving a berth come down to over-complicating matters and getting into a tangle. Just keep it simple.

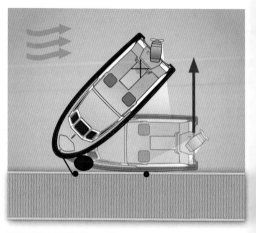

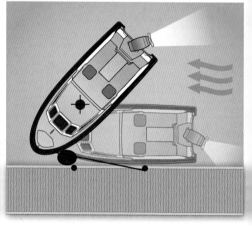

Tying up alongside a pontoon

The sides of most powerboats are too high to jump down from. Crew need to learn to lasso cleats from deck. The pontoons and walkways will rise and fall with the tide, so once set, the mooring lines will not need to be adjusted again. The lines used are a bow line, stern line and forward and stern springs which keep the boat parallel to the pontoon.

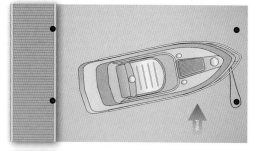

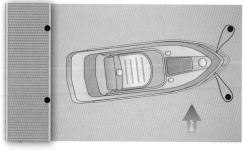

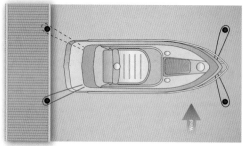

Pile/pontoon berth

- Have bow and stern lines rigged on port and starboard sides and boathook at the ready. Approach stern first slowly and lasso the windward pile first, then the leeward pile.
- Continue motoring astern to allow bowman to jump ashore.
- Tie up windward stern line first, followed by leeward stern line.
- Cross over the stern lines to act as springs and tension so that transom is clear of the pontoon or wall.

To leave:

- Set up lines so that they can be pulled through and released from onboard.
- Check which way wind and tide are running and plan departure accordingly.
- Release leeward lines first.
- Release windward bow line and engage forward gear (or astern, if you have entered the berth bow first).
- 'Walk' the boat forward past the windward pile and release bow line.
- Keep roving fenders at the ready to protect other vessels in the event of drifting down on them.

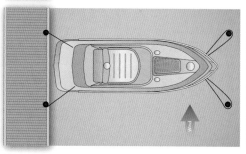

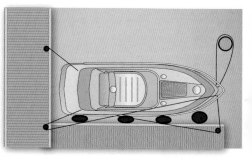

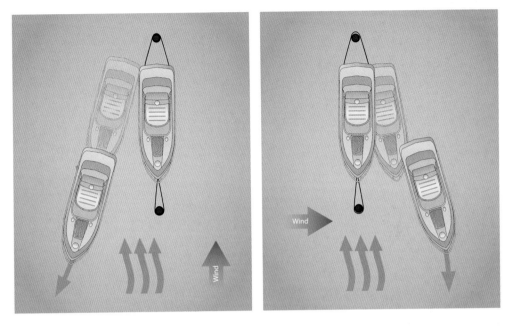

Pile moorings

- Have bow and stern lines rigged and boathook at the ready. The stern line should be flaked out so that it cannot snag when running out – this is very important.
- Approach at low speed into tide or wind, whichever is the stronger. If you are unsure, make a dummy run, first into wind and then into the tide to see which has most affect on the boat.
- As soon as possible, pass the stern line through the stern pile's sliding ring, or preferably attach it if the crewman has time, and let it run free as the boat carries on.
- As soon as possible, secure the bow line to the sliding ring on the forward pile.
- Once the boat has stopped, ease the bowline

gently while taking in the stern line and allow the boat to settle back to the desired position before securing. If conditions are difficult, lasso the stern pile, then the forward pile to secure the boat, then pass lines through the sliding rings and tie off.

To leave:

- Set up lines, including a bow spring line so that they can be pulled through and released from onboard.
- Head out stern first. Never attempt to leave down-tide.
- If there is a strong beam wind, head off away from the wind if possible to avoid being blown into the piles.

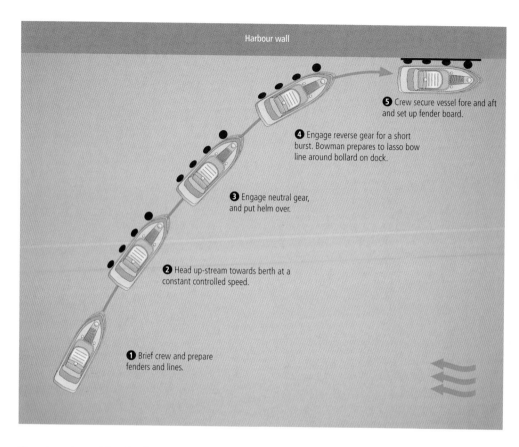

Harbour wall

5 Crew secure vessel fore and aft and set up fender board.

4 Engage reverse gear for a short burst. Bowman prepares to lasso bow line around bollard on dock.

3 Engage neutral gear, and put helm over.

2 Head up-stream towards berth at a constant controlled speed.

1 Brief crew and prepare fenders and lines.

Mooring alongside a harbour wall

- Check with harbour master or pilot notes for rise and fall of tide and any obstructions.
- Always approach into tide or wind, whichever is stronger. Use plenty of fenders to protect hull and use an outer fender board if wall is not of uniform shape.
- Moor up using separate bow/stern lines and springs.
- Warps should be at least three times the rise and fall of tide. If the tidal range is more than 9ft (3m) it may be necessary to have a crewmember on board to keep watch over the lines.

To leave:

- Set up lines so that they can be pulled through and released from onboard.
- Head out stern first using a bow spring line if space is restricted.
- Release the bow spring line when the stern has swung out and motor away.

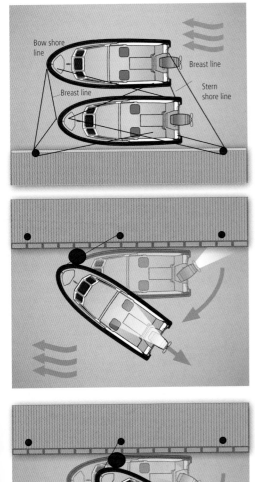

Bow shore line

Breast line

Breast line

Stern shore line

Rafting alongside other boats

- Select a boat to come alongside that is of similar or larger size to your own.
- Attach fenders at height to protect both vessels.
- Always approach into tide or wind, whichever is stronger.
- Set up bow/stern lines and springs.
- Run shorelines fore and aft to take the strain off the lines of the inside vessels.

To leave:

- Set up lines so that they can be pulled through and released from onboard.
- Head out stern first using a bow spring line if space is restricted.
- If you are the inside boat, run the down-tide line from the outer vessel around your own boat and pass to crewmember ashore.
- Motor out down tide
- Tide will help to set outer vessel back in against the wall or inner boat.
- Shore side crewmember resets shore lines, breast lines and springs.
- Boat picks up crewmember from side of outer vessel.

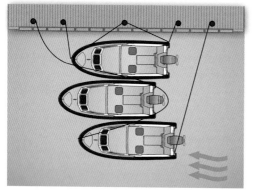

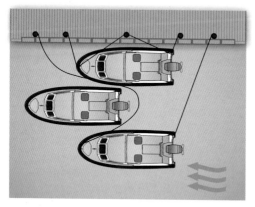

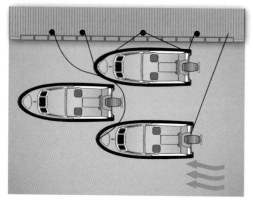

Rafting up on a buoy

Often used in busy harbours as a temporary overnight mooring for visiting boats.

- Attach fenders at a height that will protect both vessels.
- Come alongside moored vessel and attach bow line to buoy. The approach direction is given by the other vessel attached to the buoy (assuming she is of a roughly similar type) as she will be directly affected by the combined wind/tide effect at the buoy.
- Attach stern line and springs to the moored vessel.

To leave:

- Cast off and leave stern first.
- If in the midst of a group of boats, run the stern line of one vessel around the bow of your own and attach to vessel on other side.
- Reverse out, leaving one crewmember on adjacent vessel to re-tie stern and springs and pick them up from outside boat.

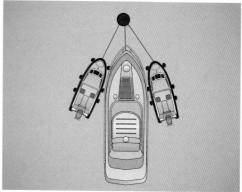

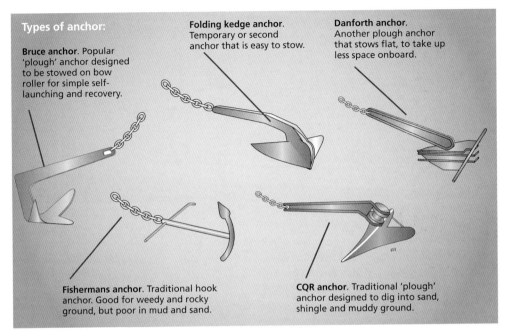

Types of anchor:

Bruce anchor. Popular 'plough' anchor designed to be stowed on bow roller for simple self-launching and recovery.

Folding kedge anchor. Temporary or second anchor that is easy to stow.

Danforth anchor. Another plough anchor that stows flat, to take up less space onboard.

Fishermans anchor. Traditional hook anchor. Good for weedy and rocky ground, but poor in mud and sand.

CQR anchor. Traditional 'plough' anchor designed to dig into sand, shingle and muddy ground.

Tripping line

It is so easy for the anchor to snag on a rock or obstruction – and just as easy to release if a tripping line was set up beforehand. Simply tie a line to the crown of the anchor, and attach a buoy or fender to the other end as a float. Then if the anchor snags, you motor up to the line and pull it onboard to retrieve the anchor upside down.

If a tripping line was not fitted, another way to release the anchor is to motor around and use the power of the vessel to pull the anchor from the opposite direction. If that fails, you have the choice of either diving down to try and release the anchor, or cutting the anchor line.

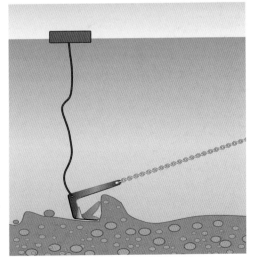

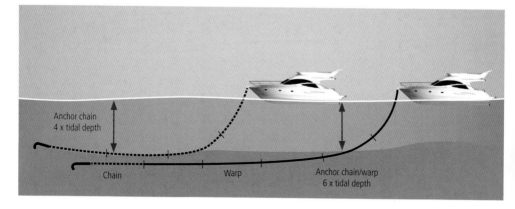

Anchor chain
4 x tidal depth

Chain

Warp

Anchor chain/warp
6 x tidal depth

Anchors work best when the pull is horizontal. The scope of chain deployed needs to be a minimum of 4 times the depth of water - and 6 times the depth when the anchor line is part chain/part warp. The chain is important. The heavier it is, the better you will sleep. Attached to the shank, it keeps the anchor lying horizontal on the bottom and takes some of the 'snatch' out of the line as the boat rides up and down on the swell. A full-length anchor chain gives most security, but where a rope anchor line is used to save weight, this requires 6–9ft (2–3m) of heavy chain attached to the anchor to weigh it down.

Paint marks on the chain or warp at 6ft (2m) distances provide a visual guide when deploying the anchor.

Using a windlass

The windlass situated on the foredeck is designed to wind the anchor chain. Some windlasses also have a smooth winch drum to control warps. These can be operated manually with a long handle, or are electric or hydraulically powered at the press of a button.

They operate under heavy load, so keep feet, fingers and loose clothing well away.

It is a good idea to clean the anchor of mud and seewead before stowing it.

Choosing an anchorage

Look for good protection from wind and swell. The anchor symbol on the chart is always a good indicator that the bottom is good holding ground. If you have any doubts about the bottom, set up a tripping line to release the anchor should it snag.

- Check the rise and fall of the tide and low water depth on the chart. Is there sufficient water below the keel? When dropping your anchor, use the depth off your echo sounder, not the depth given on the chart – it may have changed!
  Depth required to anchor = desired under keel clearance at low water + height of tide at anchoring – the next low water

- Check rise and fall at the entrance or bar. Will there be sufficient water when you plan to leave?
- Is there sufficient room to swing round with wind or tide?
- Are there any obstructions within this radius? Check by motoring around and monitor the echo sounder.
- Clear the foredeck of sails and prepare the amount of anchor chain and warp needed before dropping anchor:
  Scope required:
  4 x high water depth with chain
  6 x high water depth with chain and warp
- Snub the anchor line when fully extended with a short burst of reverse thrust to dig the anchor in.

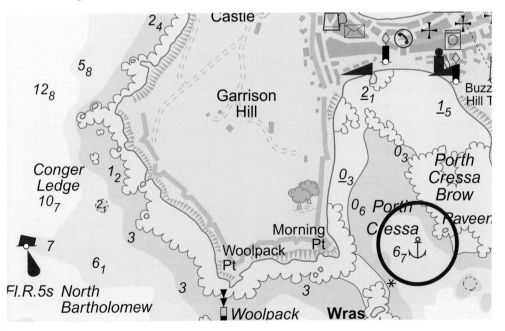

- Check the anchor is not dragging. Take bearings on prominent landmarks and check at 15-minute intervals. You can also tell if the anchor is dragging by testing for vibrations on the anchor line, which will indicate that the anchor is bumping along the bottom.

- If the anchor is dragging, pay out more scope:
  5 x high water depth with chain
  8 x high water depth with chain and warp
- If the anchor continues to drag, recover the anchor and check the chart to locate another spot to anchor.

Laying two anchors

If bad weather is predicted or you wish to limit the swing of the vessel on the tide, or in a crowded anchorage or channel, then these are times to deploy the kedge anchor.

In adverse weather, lay two anchors at 45° to the wind direction on two separate anchor cables set either side of the bows.

Scope required:
5 x high water depth with chain
8 x high water depth with chain and warp

To limit swing or maintain a set attitude to the tidal stream, deploy the second (kedge) anchor from the stern.

Clear the stern and prepare the amount of anchor chain and warp needed before dropping anchor.

Scope required:
4 x high water depth with chain
6 x high water depth with chain and warp

Pay out the bow anchor line the required distance to drop the stern anchor.

Take up on the bow anchor and cleat off. Snub the stern anchor line by hand to dig the anchor in.

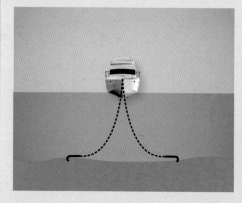
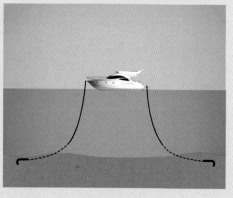

- **Picking up a mooring**
- Swing moorings provide a less expensive option to a marina berth. They usually consist of a riser chain linking the main mooring buoy to a heavy sinker or ground chain to which a string of moorings are attached, known as a 'trot'.
- If you are lucky, the main mooring buoy will have a pick-up buoy attached to a mooring strop, which is pulled onboard and secured around the bollard on the foredeck.

To pick up:
- Skipper briefs foredeck crew on approach up-tide or into wind, whichever is stronger
- Crew has boathook ready and signals angle and distance of buoy to skipper
- Crew grabs mooring strop with boathook and hauls it up to deck level
- Second crew member takes hold of pick-up buoy or strop, feeds it through bow roller, passes loop over bollard…
- …and secures the pick-up line using the OXO method around the bollard
- Some commercial moorings do not have a pick-up buoy, but simply an eye through which to attach your own mooring warp.

Pick up buoy

Bowline coiled and ready...

To pick up:

- Skipper briefs foredeck crew on approach up-tide or into wind
- Crew has boathook ready and signals angle and distance of buoy to skipper
- Second crew has mooring warp and ties off one end on bollard. If conditions allow, crew grabs eye of mooring buoy with boathook...
- ....and second crewmember passes mooring warp through eye, brings back through bow roller and ties off on bollard
- If conditions are too rough, one crewmember can lasso the buoy with a temporary mooring warp to pull it alongside for a second crewman to attach the mooring warp
- Do not leave this lasso on permanently, since it will twist up as the boat swings around the buoy and could damage the mooring

Leaving a mooring

Skipper briefs foredeck crew, which way he intends to leave.

- Skipper has engines running in neutral
- Skipper calls 'Release mooring' and crew casts off line
- Skipper allows boat to drift back on tide or wind to avoid running over mooring strop
- When clear, skipper engages forward gear and steers to clear mooring

Watch your wash. Some powerboats create a large wash when running in displacement mode. Keep speed down – below the limit if necessary.

Speed

Responsible speeding

Speed is exhilarating, but not all first-timers to boating appreciate it. Don't put them off for life! A safe speed is when you are in full control, can anticipate ahead, and your wash is not affecting others. In harbour, keep within the speed limits, and go slower if your wash is affecting moored boats. Even a moderate wash can swamp a heavily laden dinghy and make life very difficult for those trying to climb aboard their boats or working up a mast.

Check ahead before accelerating

When accelerating, the raised bow can impair vision both ahead and astern. Double check for small buoys, fishing nets and other boats around you before opening the throttles.

Keep a lookout all around

You need eyes in the back of your head to check what is going on astern and abeam, as well as ahead. Having other people around you can cause blind spots. Have them sit down and involve them as spotters, warning you of other boats and hazards around.

Murky conditions

Adjust your speed to suit the conditions. Mist and fog reduces visibility so cut your speed to allow more time to anticipate and have someone monitor the radar screen and sound the foghorn.

Keep speed down when conditions are murky too. You never know when you are going to run across a fishing boat like this one at anchor... without a radar reflector.

High speed turns

High-speed turns can be fun, but warn your crew to hold on. You won't want any of them falling overboard. Make the turn gradual and controlled, keeping the boat on the plane. If you turn too sharply, the prop will cavitate (suck in air), the revs will rise and the boat will slow right down. Pull the throttle back or widen the turn, and the prop will bite again.

Trimming the leg down before starting the turn will help maintain grip during the manoeuvre, then re-apply the power and trim out as you come out of the turn.

Save fuel

Know what the fuel consumption of your engines is. There are no fuel stations out at sea and an unscheduled detour into port will be time consuming. Run a series of timed runs at different cruising speeds in various wind and sea states and check consumption. Then write the figures in the log for future reference.

The engines will use more fuel pushing the boat into rough head seas than running with the waves. They also use a lot more fuel running flat out. Once on the plane, ease back by 500–1,000rpm and consumption will drop considerably with little noticeable difference in speed.

On twin-engined boats, equalise the engine revs by checking the rev counters or engine note.

A boat that is heavily loaded will use a lot more fuel and take longer to get on the plane. When setting out on a passage, carry a 20% safety margin of fuel in reserve.

Keep a continuous check on consumption. If you are using too much fuel, cut the throttles back to the point where the vessel is just on the plane. Look for flat water. A detour around the coastline will often be far more economic – and comfortable – than bashing into head seas straight across open water.

Think comfort...think economy!

Tides and weather

To start with, the outside elements of wind and tides can seem complex, but the telltale signs are easy to read – once you know what to look for.

As UKSA, senior instructor Richard Baggett tells his students, 'God gave you ears ... to feel which way the wind is coming from. They are the best wind antennae you have, so use them!'

The first rule before going afloat is to check the local weather forecast and tides, which are readily available from the web, weather channels, harbour offices, or sent as SMS text to your mobile/cell phone.

The second rule is to keep a weather eye out, looking for changes in wind strength or direction by monitoring flags, smoke stacks and other boats around you. The Mark 1 eyeball is an excellent forecasting tool if used regularly.

When the wind is offshore, the seas can be deceptively calm close to shore, and present strong head seas when heading back to port. Onshore winds can make it difficult to leave harbour, but once out beyond the influence of land, the waves will invariably lessen, and the wind direction will also make it much easier to return to port later.

Tidal height and flow

Over approximately 6.5 hours the height of tide rises to high water, and then over approximately the next 6.5 hours falls to low water. This happens with monotonous regularity and is predicted to the minute by tide tables which can be obtained from nautical almanacs, sailing clubs, harbour masters, and directly from the web.

Tides are caused by the interaction between the Sun, the Moon and the Earth. When the three bodies line up (with the new moon (Figure 1), or the full moon (Figure 2) the Sun's and the Moon's gravity directly add to each other, and this causes spring tides, where the high-water levels are relatively high, and the low-water levels are relatively low. Where the Sun and the Moon are at right angles relative to the Earth (half moon

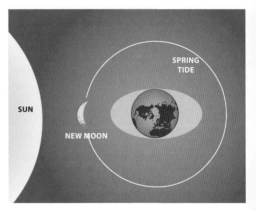

Figure 1. Gravity of Moon and Sun act together.

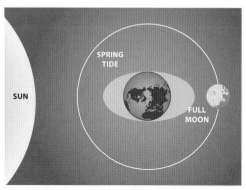

Figure 2. Gravity of Moon and Sun act together.

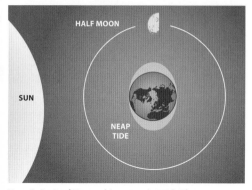

Figure 3. Gravity of Moon and Sun act against each other.

– Figure 3) their respective gravitational pulls are at right angles and therefore not directly adding to each other. This causes neap tides (Figure 5), where the high-water heights are not as high as at springs, and nor are low-water marks as low as at springs.

Apart from the obvious point that the height of tide decides which rocks present a danger, the range of tide (the difference in height between high-water and low-water on a particular day) has a direct bearing on the rate of tidal flow.

The time period of the tide is constant, so spring tides have faster rates than neap tides, because they have the same 6.5 hours to move a greater volume of water along the coast. Logically, the tide would flood in to high water, and then immediately turn and ebb towards low water.

In practice, however, the turn of tidal flow can occur up to 2 hours before the relevant high or low water. This information can be obtained from tidal stream atlases, local sailors, sailing clubs and harbour masters.

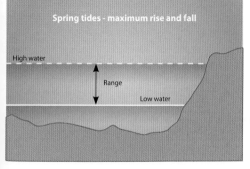

Figure 4

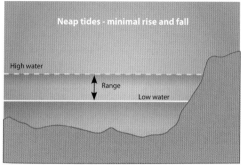

Figure 5

The combination of wind and tide

Tidal rates can vary greatly – 2 knots is fairly average in some locations, and in narrow harbour entrances or gaps between islands it can reach 5 or 6 knots on a regular basis. This has a direct effect on both the sea state and destination of the voyage.

The sea state is generated mostly by the effect of the surface wind on the water. If there is wind with tide (Figure 6), then the sea state will be relatively smooth, and not so choppy. In wind over tide (Figure 7) scenarios this can be quite different, with the waves much shorter and steeper, with a greater risk of flying spray.

If strong winds are forecast, it is important to know when the tide is flooding and ebbing, as that directly affects when the sea state goes from 'Wheeee!' to 'Heeelp!'.

Figure 6. Wind with tide.

Figure 7. Wind over tide.

Perfect sailing conditions

Idyllic conditions. Flat water translates into a smooth ride, but when the winds turn against the tidal stream, the seas become choppy and uncomfortable. Check high and low-water times and plan your day accordingly.

Clouds – what are they and what do they mean?

As air passes over water, moisture will be picked up by the air and carried in suspension. The amount of water carried and picked up depends to a large extent on the temperature of the air and the temperature of the water over which it flows. For many reasons this air may then rise or be cooled (or both) and moisture will come out of suspension in the form of water vapour, which is seen as clouds. The type of cloud formed depends on what is happening to the air from which it comes, so the clouds are a good indicator of what the weather is, or is about to be, doing.

There are four main categories of clouds:

Cirrus – a tuft or filament
Cumulus – the classic fluffy cloud
Stratus – layered cloud
Nimbus – rain-bearing cloud (usually a darker, more ominous grey)

There are many individual cloud types, the most common are as follows:

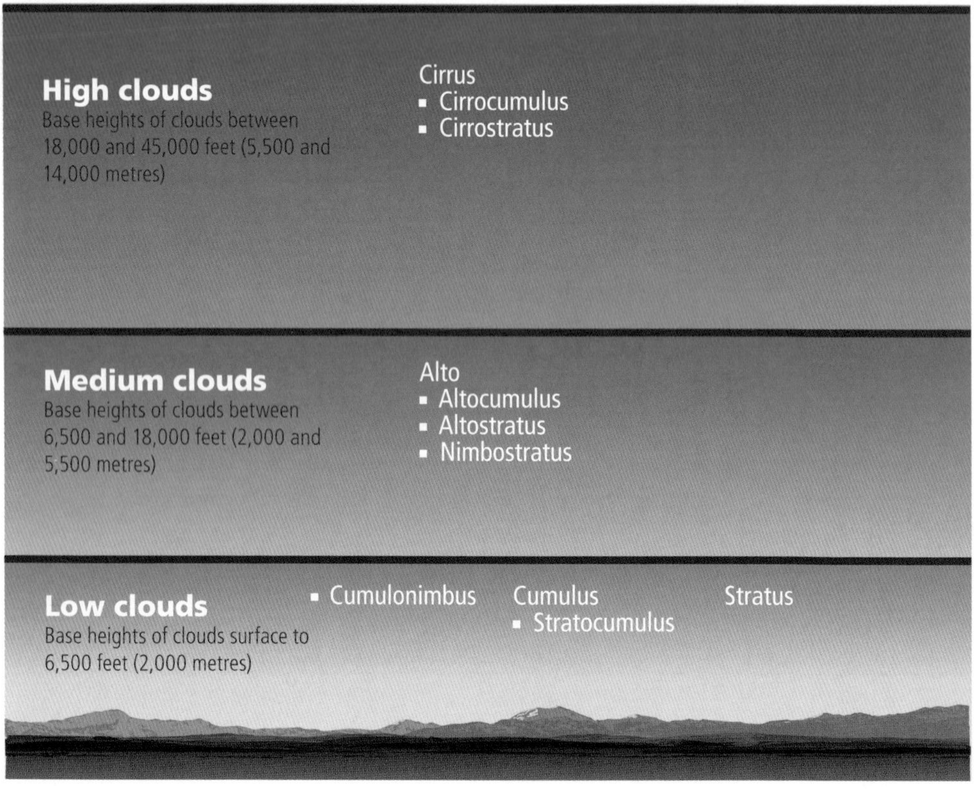

High clouds
Base heights of clouds between 18,000 and 45,000 feet (5,500 and 14,000 metres)

Cirrus
- Cirrocumulus
- Cirrostratus

Medium clouds
Base heights of clouds between 6,500 and 18,000 feet (2,000 and 5,500 metres)

Alto
- Altocumulus
- Altostratus
- Nimbostratus

Low clouds
Base heights of clouds surface to 6,500 feet (2,000 metres)

- Cumulonimbus   Cumulus   Stratus
- Stratocumulus

Cirrus: long feathery filaments of ice crystals often associated with tufts known as 'mares' tails'. These are typically associated with the approach of a frontal system, meaning that changeable weather is on the way in the next 24 hours.

Cirrocumulus: known as a 'mackerel sky' they are composed of collections of high altitude ice crystals and look like rippled sand on a beach. These are typically associated with the approach of a frontal system.

Cirrostratus: a more continuous high-level layer of ice crystals, again associated with an approaching frontal system. This cloud may give rise to a halo around the Sun and the Moon.

Altocumulus: thin, broken-up fluffy clouds. They are the next indicator after the cirrus clouds that a frontal system, and therefore rain, is on the way in the next 12 hours or so.

Altostratus: a thin, reasonably consistent layer of cloud through which the sun will shine weakly. There will be patches of darker grey in it, and this is an imminent precursor to rain and the arrival of a front.

Nimbostratus: a darker, heavier version of stratus clouds, with identifiable features that can hang off the base of the main formation almost like large sacks of rain waiting to fall. Any precipitation is likely to be heavy, with some unpredictable wind shifts and gusts on the edges of these showers.

Stratus: a most depressing low, uniform grey layer of cloud with few identifiable features. There will be scattered drizzle and light rain under these, and they generally occur at the end of fronts or in the warm sector of a frontal system.

Cumulus: individual white or light grey fluffy clouds, often seen along coastlines in the afternoon as a result of warm air rising as the day heats up or in the relatively dry air following the passing of a frontal system. They are a good indicator of fair weather.

Stratocumulus: layered cumulus clouds, generally white or light grey in patches. These are not threatening, and generally the worst that will happen is the occasional shower.

Cumulonimbus: these clouds are typically associated with cold fronts, often forming line squalls just in front of them. They are typically low based but can reach up as high as 40,000 feet (12,000 metres), and are very energetic, dark and forbidding formations, generating rain, hail, thunder and lightning, as well as unpredictable strong squalls around their edges and underneath them. They can be embedded in layers of stratocumulus and can be spotted by their extremely dark bases and characteristic anvil top.

Red sky at night, sailor's delight: this saying is often true – if a frontal system has passed over from west to east, as is generally the case, then the setting sun in the west will light up the clouds at the back of the system as it takes the rain away with it to the east.

Red sky in the morning, sailor's warning: as the rising sun in the east lights up approaching clouds in the west, the frontal system is on the way.

Beaufort Wind Scale

Force	Speed	Description	Observations
0	0–1 knots	Calm	Sea like a mirror. Smoke rises vertically.
1	1–3 knots	Light air	Ripples have appearance of scales on water. Smoke drift and flags indicate direction.
2	4–6 knots	Light breeze	Small wavelets with glassy crests. Wind can be felt on the face. Flags and wind vanes also indicate direction.
3	7–10 knots	Gentle breeze	Large wavelets. Crests begin to break producing scattered white horses. Leaves and branches begin to move. Ideal conditions to learn to sail.
4	11–16 knots	Moderate breeze	Small waves, becoming larger; frequent white horses. Keelboats require more work to keep balanced.
5	17–21 knots	Fresh winds	Moderate waves, take a more pronounced form with regular white horses formed with spray. Chance of broaching. Small trees sway in wind and flags flying horizontally.
6	22–27 knots	Strong winds	Large waves with white foam crests and spray are extensive. Limit of safety for small keelboats. Large trees sway and wind whistles.
7	28–33 knots	Near gale	Sea heaps up and white foam from breaking waves begins to be blown in streaks along the direction of the wind.
8	34–40 knots	Gale	Moderately high waves of greater length; edges of crests begin to break into spindrift. The foam is blown in well-marked streaks along the direction of the wind.

Frontal systems and weather maps

Most weather is caused by the passage of frontal systems, or depressions, or low pressure systems over the continent. A basic understanding of these and regular looks at the associated synoptic chart (the weather map) will soon allow a reasonable level of forecasting ability to be attained.

The basic source of weather is the interaction between different air masses. Broadly speaking there are four types of air mass:

Polar air masses: cold and dry air from the polar regions

Tropical air masses: warm, wet air from the tropical ocean areas

Maritime air masses: relatively wet air coming from nontropical ocean areas

Continental air masses: relatively dry air coming from large land masses

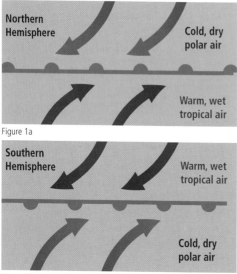

Figure 1a

Figure 1b

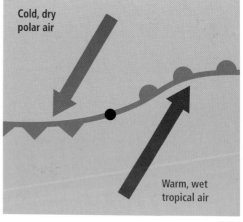

Figure 2

The frontal systems that determine most European weather are caused by the interaction of cold, dry, polar air coming from the Arctic and the warm, wet, air coming from the Atlantic.

An eddy forms (just like those seen in water running by a pontoon), and the system may start to rotate (anticlockwise in the Northern Hemisphere (Figure 1a), clockwise in the Southern (Figure 1b).

This is where two major features are formed – the warm and cold fronts. These are quite simply the front of the relatively warm and wet and relatively cold and dry air masses (Figure 2). A domestic example is the bathroom in the morning. Hot, moisture-laden air meets a cold, dry mirror, and condensation immediately forms. Warm and cold fronts are much larger versions of that, but are fundamentally down to the meeting of two different air masses. The section of air between the two fronts is the relatively warm and wet air mass, known as the warm sector.

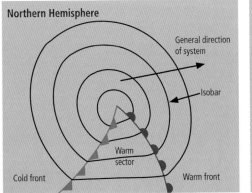

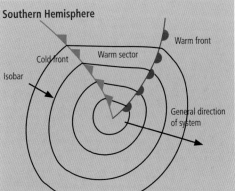

Figure 3

With the frontal system fully developed and usually moving to the north-east or east, there is a complete circulation around the centre of the low, just as in little whirlpools on the edge of a fast flowing stream. This can be seen in terms of a pressure map, otherwise known as a synoptic chart (Figure 3).

Here, the warm and cold fronts are represented, and the shape of the system as a whole is shown by the isobars, or lines of equal pressure. These isobars are the first forecasting tool, as the wind direction is generally about 10 to 15° off the line of the isobar, offset inwards towards the centre of the low. Wind strength is directly related to the spacing between the isobars (the pressure gradient Figure 4). The closer the isobars, the more the pressure gradient, and therefore the stronger the wind. Once the wind direction and strength have been looked at, the weather is next. This is driven by what is happening in the air above the boat.

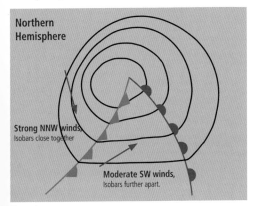

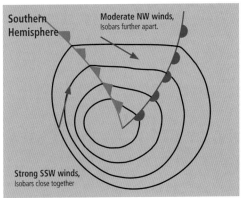

Figure 4

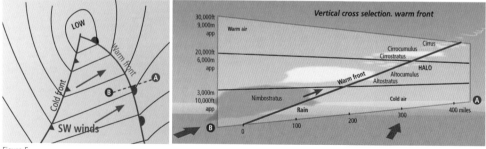

Figure 5

As the front goes over, the rain will reach its maximum, and the visibility will drop. Once the front has passed, the rain will ease up, and the visibility will improve, but not back to how it was before the front, as the warm sector air mass is relatively warm and wet and so will hold more moisture and not be as clear (Figure 5). The cloud cover will be mostly stratus or nimbostratus, and there may be fairly steady rain. The wind will have veered, and will be reasonably constant in strength and direction.

The cold front is a very different animal to the warm front. As the air mass is cold and dry, it cannot climb up and over the warm sector air mass, so all the interaction between the two air masses happens in almost the same vertical plane, potentially allowing the formation of massive cumulonimbus clouds (Figure 6). The conditions under the front are potentially dangerous, with unpredictable squalls coming off the edges of the cumulonimbus clouds. Heavy rain or hail and electrical storms are possible. As a result of all this, visibility may be very poor.

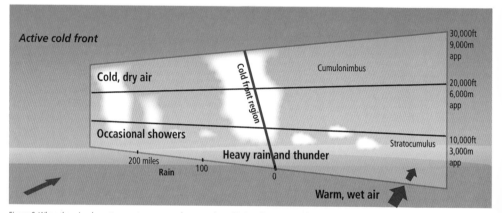

Figure 6. When there is a large temperature contrast between the cold air and warm air, violent weather can be expected along the cold front, with rain squalls and perhaps hail and thunder.

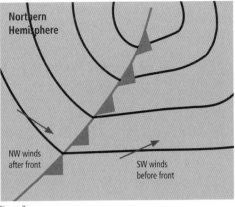

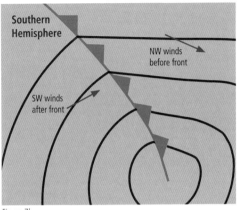

Figure 7a

Figure 7b

After the cold front has passed, the wind will veer again, the skies will clear almost immediately, and as the air is now part of the cold, dry mass. Visibility will be excellent often with some scenic cumulus clouds (Figure 7).

As the whole system becomes more mature the cold front will start to catch up with the warm front, very much like a zipper being done up. This forms an occluded front and results in what's left of the warm sector being pushed up above the preceding and following cold air masses which now join up (Figure 8).

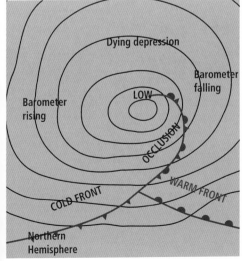

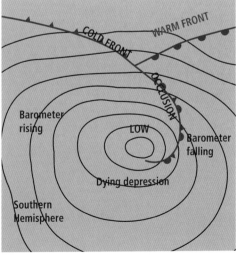

Figure 8a

Figure 8b

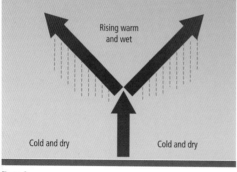

Figure 9

Atlantic or Azores High. They are not as mobile as low-pressure systems, and are also generally composed of just one air mass, and so do not have the fronts associated with a low. In the Northern Hemisphere they rotate clockwise (anticlockwise in the Southern Hemisphere) and are represented by isobars as with low pressure systems.

The same rules apply for wind strength and direction as before – the direction of the isobars is broadly speaking the direction of the wind around the high, with the wind offset by 10 to 15 degrees away from the centre of it. The wind strength is governed by the spacing in between the isobars, the pressure gradient.

High-pressure systems can bring balmy weather, and in European waters over summer this is often the case, with the centre of a high sitting over northern France bringing light and variable winds to most of the European continent.

However, if a relatively static high acts as a buffer for a strong low (Figure 10), then very large pressure gradients can occur between the

As all this warm wet air is lifted, it cools, causing moisture to come out of the air in the form of a persistent, miserable drizzle and low-level cloud. (Figure 9). Since this is towards the end of the frontal system's life, it's normally not very energetic.

High-pressure systems and their interaction with low-pressure systems

High-pressure systems are generally found over large ocean masses, for example the North

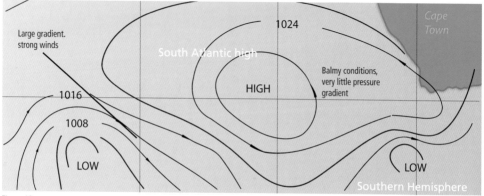

Figure 10

systems, causing very strong winds, as illustrated, for the Southern Hemisphere.

Fog

Fog is basically sea level cloud, and is caused in two ways: radiation or land fog. This occurs either when there is not much gradient wind, there is a change in sea temperature or a drop in wind speed. A high-pressure system overhead is an ideal circumstance.

During the day the air will heat up over the shore and over the sea, and moisture will be taken in by the air as it heats up (Figure 11). As soon as the sun goes down, the air will cool and start to release this moisture in the form of fog. It will collect in low lying areas, e.g. harbours and river valleys, and will occasionally spill out up to two or three miles from land. When the sun rises, the air will heat up again, the moisture will go back into suspension, and the fog will clear – this is what is meant by the sun 'burning off' the fog. So, if at breakfast there is no visibility and little wind, then by about 1100 the fog will have gone and sailing will be possible (depending on the wind).

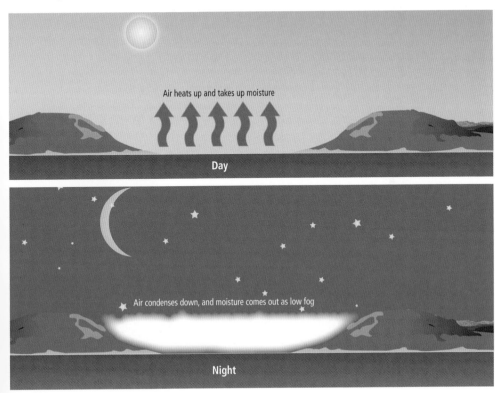

Air heats up and takes up moisture

Day

Air condenses down, and moisture comes out as low fog

Night

Figure 11

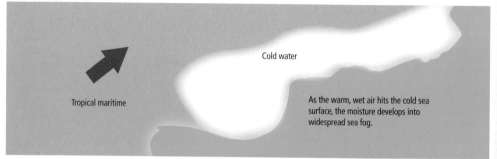

Cold water

Tropical maritime

As the warm, wet air hits the cold sea surface, the moisture develops into widespread sea fog.

Figure 12

After the sun goes down, the air cools, releasing moisture, which develops into night fog (Figure 12).

Advection, or sea fog

This is caused by relatively warm, wet air blowing over cold water. The cold sea surface cools the surface air, causing the moisture to come out of suspension as fog. This occurs mostly in the spring, when water temperature is coldest after winter and the tropical maritime air masses are being brought in from warmer latitudes (Figure 13).

This fog is more difficult to shift. An increase in wind speed just brings in more moisture, and sea fog can still be there in strong winds. Because new moisture is being brought in constantly, the sun cannot heat up the air sufficiently. The only way sea fog can dissipate is when there is a change in moisture, temperature or wind (Figure 13).

Visibility	
Good	More than 5 miles (9.25km)
Moderate	2–5 miles (3.7–9.25km)
Poor	0.5–2 miles (1–3.7km)
Fog	Less than 0.5mile (1km)

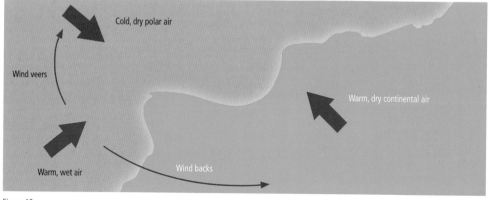

Cold, dry polar air

Wind veers

Warm, dry continental air

Warm, wet air

Wind backs

Figure 13

Weather terms

Barometric tendency – The rise or fall of the barometer at three-hour intervals, giving an early indication to a change in the weather.

Cyclonic – Term often used in shipping forecasts when a low is tracking through a sea area and wind shifts are difficult to predict.

Depressions – Rotating frontal systems.

Front – The front edge of a relatively warm, wet air mass (for a warm front) or a relatively cold, dry air mass (for a cold front).

Gradient wind – The wind caused by pressure difference. Wind flowing from high and low pressure, which is affected by the rotation of the Earth's surface, causing it to blow around high and low-pressure systems. The closer the isobars, the stronger the wind.

Gusts – Parcels of fast-moving air sucked down by rising thermal currents, which last for several minutes. Strong gusts occur when the descending upper wind is reinforced by down draughts on the surface generated by heavy rain and thunderstorms.

Line squall – A cold front often marked by a line of low black cloud, which brings with it a sharp rise in wind speed and direction for a short term.

Mistral – Localized strong to gale force wind. This particular wind refers to the predictable slope wind that blows down the Rhône Valley and extends out across the Rhône delta into the Gulf of Lions. Forecasters can usually predict its passage to within minutes. This phenomena occurs in many parts of the world. It is known as the Meltemi in the Aegean Sea, Tramontana or Garigliano on the west coast of Italy and northern Corsica, and the Hamatan off West Africa.

Troughs – Frontal troughs are easily recognisable as a line of changing weather. Non-frontal troughs are harder to pick up, as the air mass does not change discernibly as the front passes through. However, the pressure falls ahead and rises behind and winds back ahead and veer behind. Troughs often follow a cold front and rotate around a depression like the spokes of a wheel.

Veering and backing winds – A veering wind changes direction in a clockwise direction and a backing wind moves anticlockwise.

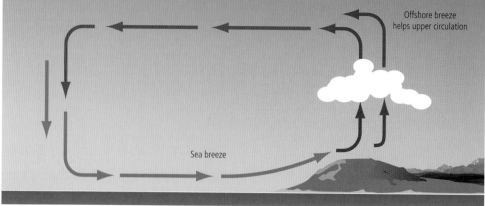

Figure 14

Sea breezes

Sea breezes can transform hot, balmy summer days into quite rough weather inshore. They are caused by the difference in warming characteristics between land and sea (Figure 14).

The land will heat up faster than the sea, and so the air above the land will heat up faster than that above the sea. This makes it expand and rise up. As it expands upwards, it also expands outwards, and pushes out to sea. As there is now physically less air over the land and more air over the sea, a localised low pressure is formed over the land, and a localised high pressure is formed over the sea, which causes a sea level breeze – the sea breeze – to start blowing from the sea towards the shore.

As the afternoon wears on, the continual rising of moisture laden air above the land will cause cumulus clouds to form along the coast. Also, if there is a slight offshore high level wind, this helps the development of the sea breeze.

Wind shadows and funnelling

These two effects are entirely local, and are a function of large obstructions around and through which the wind has to pass.

Any tall object, such as a moored cargo ship or a large headland, will have a wind shadow on its leeward side (Figure 15). This wind shadow of an obstruction will be approximately 6 times its height. By looking for ripples on the water it is often possible to see where the wind shadow finishes, and to plan your route accordingly.

Tips

❶ Know your limitations.

❷ Always get a forecast for the time you intend to sail, plus some extra days.

❸ Always tell someone where you are going and when you intend to be back.

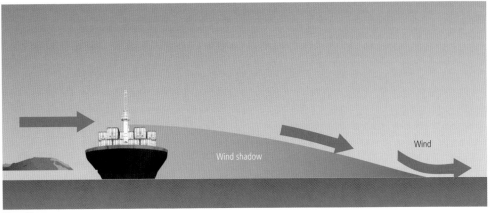

Figure 15

When cruising in estuaries or harbours with tall buildings nearby, there will be alleys between these obstructions where the wind will be funnelled, causing very sudden and local areas of increased and possibly shifted wind (Figure 16). Again, by keeping an eye open for the change in surface ripples caused by a change in wind characteristics, some warning can be had. Another sign will be vessels in front of you suddenly heeling heavily while sailing upwind, or broaching out of control when sailing downwind.

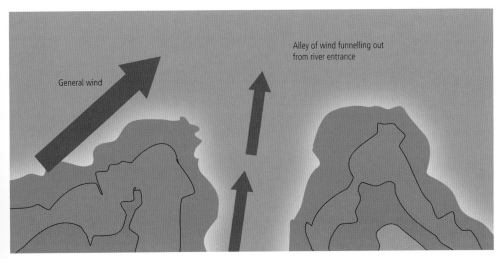

Figure 16

Basics of navigation

Nautical charts – there is no substitute

Most powerboats are equipped with a chart plotter and GPS, and once way points have been plotted, it becomes a simple case of following the line.... Or is it?

But what if there is an electrics failure onboard, or the American military suddenly pull the plug on their satellites, as they have in the past? Have you the skills to navigate using charts, and how good is your dead reckoning? For those who rely exclusively on electronic charts, it's time to get back to basics.

A chart catalogue highlights the coverage of each chart and its number. The UK Hydrographic Office produces standard charts for every part of the world. NOAA's Office of Coastal Survey does the same for the coastal waters of the US and its territories. There are also small-craft charts designed for use on smaller chart tables. Using electronic charts is fine, but always carry a paper chart as back up – just in case.

Chart projections

Projection is a way to present the globe as a flat chart. A Gnomonic projection is used for ocean charts and shows the world in 3D, while the Mercator projection, which is commonly used for coastal charts, shows the lines of longitude in parallel. Imagine a sheet of paper wrapped around the Earth, touching around the equator. If you turn on bright light at the centre of the planet, the shadows of the land masses and lines of latitude and longitude will be projected on this paper. This Mercator projection converts the constant bearing lines around the globe into straight lines on the charts. These are known as rhumb lines.

Charts must be kept up to date. Minor corrections will be found in weekly updates published as 'Notices to Mariners' **www.nga.mil** for all US issued charts; **www.nmwebsearch.com** for all UK issued charts. When major corrections are made, publishers will issue a new edition. Electronic charts can be updated online or with a CD ROM. Pilot books and nautical almanacs provide detailed information about ports, including tidal heights, streams, pilotage notes and contact information for marinas and harbour authorities: **www.wileynautical.com** for the Thames, English Channel and adjacent coasts; **http://asa.usno.navy.mil** for an astronomical nautical almanac; **http://aa.usno.navy.mil** for a US nautical almanac.

This gives the most familiar chart, where the latitude scale 'stretches' the further north or south you are from the equator.

With further manipulation the final projection is as shown on the left.

The two projections (right) are 'cylindrical' projections, as they effectively wrap a cylinder around the globe.

One common 'zenithal' projection is the gnomonic projection shown here, which is used for ocean navigation.

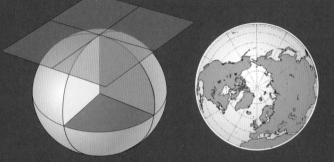

Title information on charts

This is very important, as it defines what units are used for measurement, how you plot positions on the chart and where the actual chart data comes from, as well as important information specific to the charted area.

As an example, let's look at Admiralty Chart 1400, the Outer Approaches to Puerto Cristóbal on the north coast of Panama, printed in 2006.

Depths: These are given in metres. Many charts are still in fathoms and feet, so do check. Charts outside European waters often refer to 'Mean Lower Low Water' (MLLW). This is similar to 'Mean Low Water Springs', and a table is provided on the chart.

Heights: Areas of drying heights, i.e. parts of the seabed that are not always covered by the sea, are marked in green, with the actual drying height above Chart Datum underlined, as shown below.

Other heights, for example the heights of lights and the clearance of bridges and power cables, are specified for each chart. In this case, it is above Mean High Higher Water, on other charts it is Mean High Water Springs, and on charts printed after 2004, it may be Highest Astronomical Tide. This is important to check.

Positions: In this case the chart is a World Geodetic System chart (WGS84), so GPS positions on this datum can be plotted directly onto it. This is not always the case – so do check it.

Navigational marks: IALA B in this case – 'red right return' (See page 121). If the Americas are your first landfall since leaving Europe, this may come as a surprise.

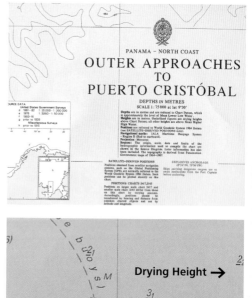

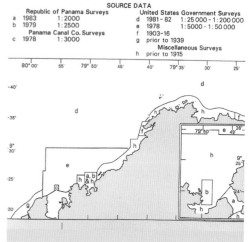

Drying Height →

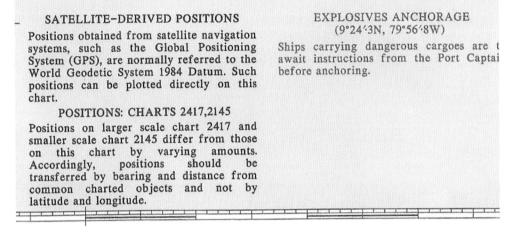

SATELLITE-DERIVED POSITIONS

Positions obtained from satellite navigation systems, such as the Global Positioning System (GPS), are normally referred to the World Geodetic System 1984 Datum. Such positions can be plotted directly on this chart.

POSITIONS: CHARTS 2417,2145

Positions on larger scale chart 2417 and smaller scale chart 2145 differ from those on this chart by varying amounts. Accordingly, positions should be transferred by bearing and distance from common charted objects and not by latitude and longitude.

EXPLOSIVES ANCHORAGE
(9°24´3N, 79°56´8W)

Ships carrying dangerous cargoes are t await instructions from the Port Captai before anchoring.

Other information: On each chart there will be local information, for example, the explosives anchorage detailed here. If you have not been to this area before it is important to read this thoroughly.

Projection: With a Mercator chart you can measure bearings directly.

Sources: Very important. Not all the survey data is recent, as shown above. Here, the most recent data is from 1983 with some areas not surveyed since 1915, and if the bottom is coral or sand, as opposed to rock, it may have changed dramatically.

Chart corrections

Paper charts must be kept up-to-date with changes published in the weekly *Notices to Mariners* (see page 108). Corrections applied to charts should be made in magenta pen and then added to the bottom left corner of the chart. You should also carry an inventory of the charts on board and catalogue the corrections that have been applied.

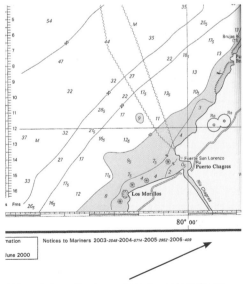

Add new chart corrections in magenta pen here and note the year

Latitude and longitude

All meridians of longitude are great circles, meaning they cut the earth exactly in half between the Poles. Meridians of longitude are marked 180° West and 180° East from the Greenwich Meridian, now known as Universal Time Coefficient (UTC), due to the fact that the French pay for the nuclear clocks from which time is measured. Latitude is measured from the Equator, 90° North and 90° South; the Equator is the only great circle in the parallels of latitude.

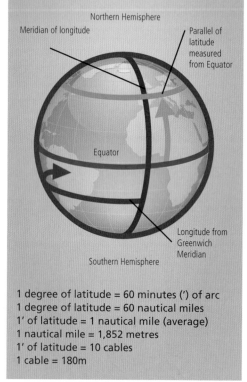

Northern Hemisphere
Meridian of longitude
Parallel of latitude measured from Equator
Equator
Longitude from Greenwich Meridian
Southern Hemisphere

1 degree of latitude = 60 minutes (') of arc
1 degree of latitude = 60 nautical miles
1' of latitude = 1 nautical mile (average)
1 nautical mile = 1,852 metres
1' of latitude = 10 cables
1 cable = 180m

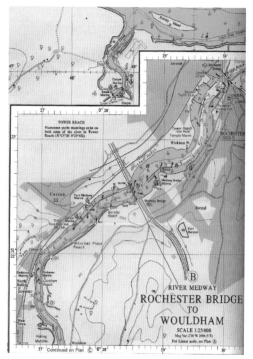

RIVER MEDWAY
ROCHESTER BRIDGE
TO
WOULDHAM
SCALE 1:25 000

Reading positions

The latitude comes from the vertical axis, i.e. north/south, and longitude comes from the horizontal axis, i.e. east/west, shown above.

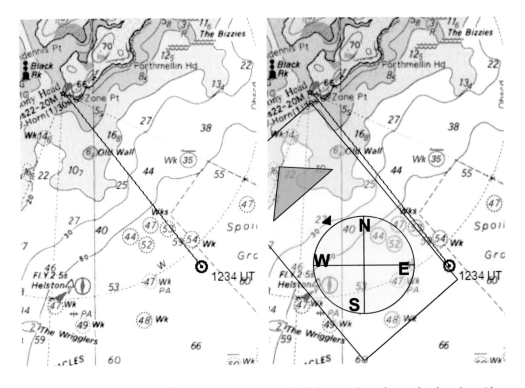

Measuring a course on a chart

This is a fundamental chart function, and starts by drawing a line from the place where you want to take the bearing toward the place you want to take the bearing to.

In this example, if you've put a fix on the chart at 1234UT (the log reading is in brackets) and want to find the bearing of St Anthony Head lighthouse in order to be able to identify it on the shore, draw a line from your position to the lighthouse.

Then put your plotter on the chart parallel to the line you've drawn with the big arrow on the main part of the plotter pointing towards

the lighthouse, i.e. along the bearing. Line up the circular bearing wheel at the centre of the plotter so that the N/S line on that wheel lines up with a convenient N/S line on the chart, and read off the bearing – in this case 322° (true).

Always ask yourself if this makes sense – at 0230 it can be easy to get things 180° out, but by saying '322° – that's roughly NW – that looks right, I know Falmouth's roughly that way' you can save yourself a lot of mistakes. Had you got it 180° out, it would have been '142° – that's roughly SE – hang on – that's where France is!'.

Measuring distances

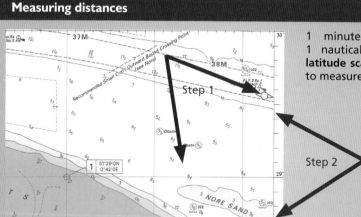

1 minute of latitude is 1 nautical mile – so the **latitude scale** is **always** used to measure **distance**.

Step 1: Use your dividers to scribe off the distance to be measured, in this case between the 5.5m depth Obstruction & the Reach No 1 buoy.

Step 2: Keeping the dividers at the same width (you need a set which is stiff enough to hold a setting, but not so stiff you can't move them), move them to the latitude scale, and measure the distance – in this case 0.55 nautical miles.

Be careful to measure distances at roughly the same latitude at which you first measure them – due to the Mercator projection of a 3D globe onto a 2D chart, the scale will change as the latitude changes. Try it on a chart that covers 50 miles or more.

Electronic navigation techniques

Satellite navigation systems are now widely available, and standard on most powerboats. The most common system is the Global Positioning System (GPS), which allows you to navigate to an accuracy of a few metres anywhere in the world.

Each individual set will have its own specific operating instructions, and this section deals with how you use the data from the instrument, not on the specific operating methods.

VERY IMPORTANT

It is **vital** that the datum used by the chart you are working on is the same as the datum used by your GPS set (see page 126). If these are not the same, significant and dangerous navigational errors can occur. Similarly, some of the most beautiful parts of the world (Indian Ocean, Caribbean and South Pacific islands) have significant chart datum differences. **Always back up close quarters GPS with visual and radar fixes.**

Basic GPS outputs and their derivatives

GPS sets directly measure position and the way that position changes. The basic outputs are:

Position: Latitude and longitude

SOG: Speed over ground

COG: Course over ground

You can input waypoints to the GPS set, and set it to navigate between them as a route.

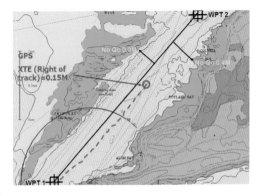

Derived from this are:

DTG: Distance to go to next waypoint or end of route.

BTW: Bearing to next waypoint. This can be set to degrees True or Magnetic.

TTG: Time to go to next waypoint or end of route. This is usually derived from DTG and VMG, and is an instantaneous reading, not an average one.

XTE: Cross track error with respect to the ideal track between waypoints. On the screen below, the XTE is being monitored either side of the ideal track.

Using GPS data efficiently

Position fixing can be done in several ways. There is obviously the direct transposition of latitude and longitude onto the chart, but there are several faster ways of doing it.

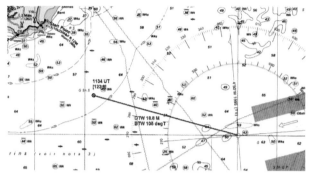

Distance and bearing to waypoint

The centre of the nearest compass rose is ideal for this. By plotting the bearing and distance to waypoint you can get a fix with only one plotter line – very efficient and quick. The waypoint doesn't have to be one you are actually travelling to, but one that your GPS is programmed to give data relative to.

Electronic charts

The logical step from using your GPS data on a paper chart is to feed it directly into an electronic chart, and get a continuous up-to-date plot of where you are. This is really convenient, but it is vital to keep a regular log entry going, because if the technology fails, you need to be able to move back to paper from your last known point.

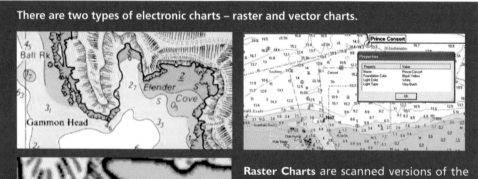

There are two types of electronic charts – raster and vector charts.

Raster Charts are scanned versions of the paper charts, and when you zoom in you actually move from chart to more detailed chart. If you zoom in too far you just get a fuzzy screen.

Vector Charts have layered data – as you zoom in more and more data is revealed. Each individual feature has data about it stored in the chart, giving you a lot of useful pilotage information.

Buoys, lights and how to use them

Light characteristics

Lighthouses are generally the most complex of these. A lighthouse could have the characteristic:

Oc.WR.15s.23m.22-20M
Horn(1)30s

This means it is **Oc**culting, (a rhythmic light where the duration of light in each period is longer than the duration of darkness) has **W**hite & **R**ed sectors, repeating every **15s**, the main lamp is **23m** above Mean High Water Springs (MHWS), the White is visible for **22** nautical miles, the Red **20**. In restricted visibility, it will sound a **horn** – once every **30s**.

Isolated danger marks

Safe water marks

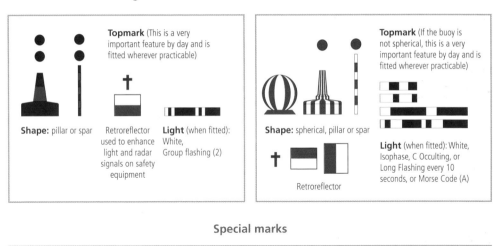

Topmark (This is a very important feature by day and is fitted wherever practicable)

Shape: pillar or spar

Retroreflector used to enhance light and radar signals on safety equipment

Light (when fitted): White, Group flashing (2)

Topmark (If the buoy is not spherical, this is a very important feature by day and is fitted wherever practicable)

Shape: spherical, pillar or spar

Retroreflector

Light (when fitted): White, Isophase, C Occulting, or Long Flashing every 10 seconds, or Morse Code (A)

Special marks

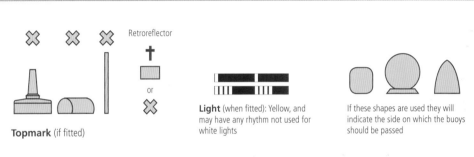

Retroreflector

Topmark (if fitted)

or

Light (when fitted): Yellow, and may have any rhythm not used for white lights

If these shapes are used they will indicate the side on which the buoys should be passed

Light Characters Light Characters on Light Buoys ---> IQ			
Abbreviation		Class of Light	Illustration Period shown
International	National		
		Fixed	
Occulting (total duration of light longer than total duration of darkness)			
Oc	Occ	Single-occulting	
Oc(2)	GpOcc(2)	Group-occulting	
Oc(2+3)	GpOcc(2+3)	Composite group-occulting	
Isophase (duration of light and darkness equal)			
Iso	Isophase		
Flashing (total duration of light shorter than total duration of darkness)			
Fl		Single-flashing	
Fl(3)	GpFl(3)	Group-flashing	
Fl(2+1)	GpFl(2+1)	Composite group-flashing	
L Fl		Long-flashing	
Quick (repetition rate of 50 to 79 – usually either 50 or 60 flashes per minute)			
Q	QkFl	Continuous quick	
Q(3)	QkFl(3)	Group quick	
IQ	IntQkFl	Interrupted quick	
Very quick (repetition rate of 80 to 159 – usually either 100 or 120 flashes per minute)			
VQ	VQkFl	Continuous very quick	
VQ(3)	VQkFl(3)	Group very quick	
IVQ	IntVkFl	Interrupted very quick	
Ultra quick (repetition rate of 160 or more – usually 240 to 300 flashes per minute)			
UQ		Continuous ultra quick	
IUQ		Group ultra quick	
Mo(K)		Morse Code	
FFl		Fixed and flashing	
Al.WR	Alt.Wr	Alternating	

Region A

This diagram is schematic and in the case of pillar buoys in particular, their features will vary with the individual design of the buoys in use.

PORT HAND
Colour: Red.
Shape: Can, pillar or spar.
Topmark (when fitted):
Single red can.
Retroreflector: Red
band or square.

PORT HAND
Colour: Red.
Shape: Can, pillar or spar.
Topmark (when fitted):
Single red can.
Retroreflector: Red
band or square.

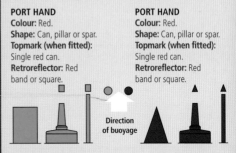

Direction of buoyage

LIGHTS, when fitted, may have any rhythm other than composite group flashing (2+ I) used on modified lateral marks indicating a preferred channel. Examples are:

O.R		Continuous-quick light		O.G
Fl.R		Single-flashing light		Fl.G
LFl.R		Long-flashing light		LFl.G
Fl(2)R		Group-flashing light		Fl(2)G

The lateral colours of red or green are frequently used for minor shore lights, such as those marking pier heads and the extremities of jetties.

Preferred channel to starboard
Colour: Red with one
broad green band.
Shape: Can, pillar or spar.
Topmark (when fitted):
Single red can.
Retroreflector:
Red band or square.

Preferred channel to port
Colour: Green with one
broad red band.
Shape: Conical, pillar or spar.
Topmark (when fitted): Single
green cone point upward.
Retroreflector:
Green band or triangle.

Direction of buoyage

Fl(2+1)R	Composite group flashing (2+ I) light	Fl(2+ 1)G

Where port or starboard marks do not rely on can or conical buoy shapes for identification, they carry the appropriate topmark where practicable or lettered, the numbering or lettering follows the conventional direction of buoyage. Special marks, with can and conical shapes but painted yellow, may be used in conjunction with the standard lateral marks for special types of channel.

Region B

This diagram is schematic and in the case of pillar buoys in particular, their features will vary with the individual design of the buoys in use.

PORT HAND
Colour: Red.
Shape: Can, pillar or spar.
Topmark (when fitted):
Single red can.
Retroreflector: Red
band or square.

PORT HAND
Colour: Red.
Shape: Can, pillar or spar.
Topmark (when fitted):
Single red can.
Retroreflector: Red
band or square.

Direction of buoyage

LIGHTS, when fitted, may have any rhythm other than composite group flashing (2+ I) used on modified lateral marks indicating a preferred channel. Examples are:

O.R		Continuous-quick light		O.G
Fl.R		Single-flashing light		Fl.G
LFl.R		Long-flashing light		LFl.G
Fl(2)R		Group-flashing light		Fl(2)G

The lateral colours of red or green are frequently used for minor shore lights, such as those marking pier heads and the extremities of jetties.

Preferred channel to starboard
Colour: Red with one
broad green band.
Shape: Can, pillar or spar.
Topmark (when fitted):
Single red can.
Retroreflector:
Red band or square.

Preferred channel to port
Colour: Green with one
broad red band.
Shape: Conical, pillar or spar.
Topmark (when fitted): Single
green cone, point upward.
Retroreflector: Green
band or triangle.

Direction of buoyage

Fl(2+1)R	Composite group flashing (2+ I) light	Fl(2+ 1)G

Where port or starboard marks do not rely on can or conical buoy shapes for identification, they carry the appropriate topmark where practicable, or lettered, the numbering or lettering follows the conventional direction of buoyage. Special marks, with can and conical shapes but painted yellow, may be used in conjunction with the standard lateral marks for special types of channel.

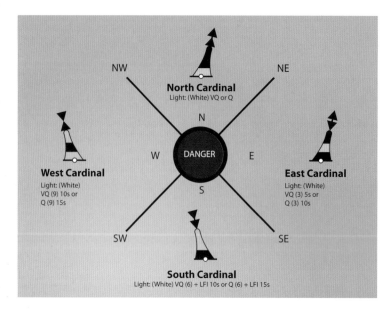

NW

North Cardinal
Light: (White) VQ or Q

NE

N

W · DANGER · E

S

West Cardinal
Light: (White)
VQ (9) 10s or
Q (9) 15s

East Cardinal
Light: (White)
VQ (3) 5s or
Q (3) 10s

SW

SE

South Cardinal
Light: (White) VQ (6) + LFl 10s or Q (6) + LFl 15s

Cardinal marks are used to tell you which side to leave dangers. For example, stay north of a North Cardinal mark to be safe.

The direction of buoyage

The direction of buoyage is shown by a large magenta arrow at various points on the chart.

This defines which side is port and starboard hand for the lateral markers when it is not obvious from the shape of the land.

The relationship between the chart and the way you interpret the buoys in the IALA-A and B regions is as shown opposite.

Direction of Buoyage

Buoyage

Depending where you are in the world the lateral markers, i.e. port and starboard hand markers, will be either the **IALA-A** or **IALA-B** system.

IALA-A is used by nations in Europe, Australia, New Zealand, parts of Africa and most of Asia other than the Philippines, Japan and Korea.

IALA-B is used by nations in North America, Central America and South America, the Philippines, Japan and Korea.

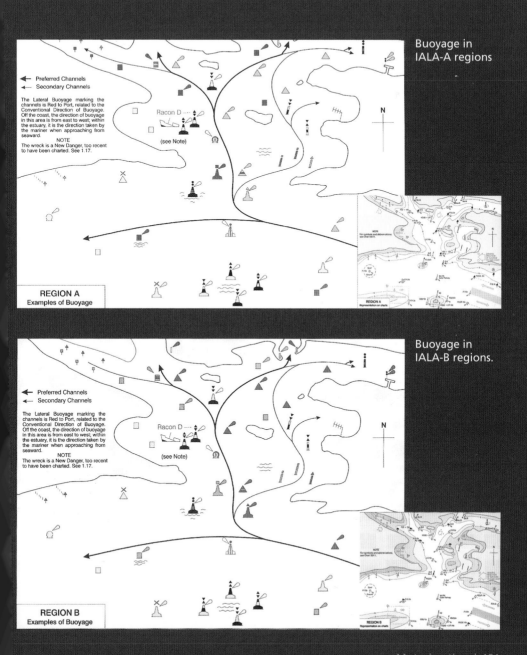

Buoyage in
IALA-A regions

Preferred Channels
Secondary Channels

The Lateral Buoyage marking the
channels is Red to Port, related to the
Conventional Direction of Buoyage.
Off the coast, the direction of buoyage
in this area is from east to west; within
the estuary, it is the direction taken by
the mariner when approaching from
seaward.

NOTE
The wreck is a New Danger, too recent
to have been charted. See 1.17.

Racon D

(see Note)

N

REGION A
Examples of Buoyage

Buoyage in
IALA-B regions.

Preferred Channels
Secondary Channels

The Lateral Buoyage marking the
channels is Red to Port, related to the
Conventional Direction of Buoyage.
Off the coast, the direction of buoyage
in this area is from east to west; within
the estuary, it is the direction taken by
the mariner when approaching from
seaward.

NOTE
The wreck is a New Danger, too recent
to have been charted. See 1.17.

Racon D

(see Note)

N

REGION B
Examples of Buoyage

Compass corrections

Magnetic compasses point to the magnetic north pole, but have some errors which have to be accounted for. These are magnetic **variation** (a global effect) and **deviation** (particular to each vessel).

Magnetic variation

Early mariners assumed that any compass pointed towards the North Pole and it was not until the early nineteenth century that navigators found that there are two north poles. The Magnetic North Pole is in Arctic Canada (82.7°N 114.4°W moving in a northwesterly direction in 2005). This angle between the True North and Magnetic North Poles has to be accounted for precisely. This correction angle is called Magnetic Variation.

There is similar variation between the South Magnetic Pole at approximately 64°S, 138°E, so if variation is west, then your compass needle points to the west of True North.

On Admiralty charts the size and change in time of the magnetic field is represented by a **compass rose**. The outer ring is aligned with True North and the inner ring with Magnetic North for the given year, in this case 2007. To calculate the variation for any given year, say 2009, you need to do the following:

12° 00'W 2007 (10'E) means that in 2007, the variation was exactly 12°W, decreasing by 10' annually, i.e. moving eastward by 10'E every year.
Variation in 2007 = 12° 00'W
Annual change = 10'E
2 year's worth = 20'E
Variation in 2009 = 11° 40'W

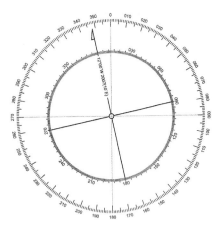

For yachting purposes, round this to the nearest degree.

Magnetic deviation

This is caused by ferrous items like the engine, which create local distortions to the magnetic field near each compass. This effect changes with the vessel's heading, since the relative positions of the metal object and the compass change within the magnetic field. It is good practice (and mandatory for commercially operated vessels) to have the compass checked and if necessary adjusted annually by a qualified compass adjuster. This is known as swinging the compass, and usually takes no more than a couple of hours.

The graph shows how deviation changes with the vessel's heading, and also how the deviation card, or compass card, is always a sinusoid. A good compass adjuster working with a good compass can get the deviation down to less than a couple of degrees.

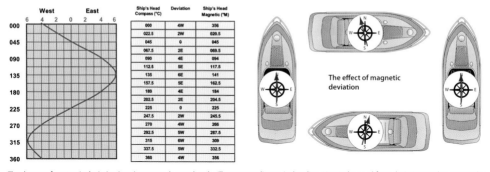

Ship's Head Compass (°C)	Deviation	Ship's Head Magnetic (°M)
000	4W	356
022.5	2W	020.5
045	0	045
067.5	2E	069.5
090	4E	094
112.5	5E	117.5
135	6E	141
157.5	5E	162.5
180	4E	184
202.5	2E	204.5
225	0	225
247.5	2W	245.5
270	4W	266
292.5	5W	287.5
315	6W	309
337.5	5W	332.5
360	4W	356

The effect of magnetic deviation

The degree of magnetic deviation is unique to each vessel and will vary according to its heading. Hence the need for a deviation card to correct the compass readings.

Applying compass corrections

There are three type of compass heading:

Degrees True: with respect to **True North** – you put this on and measure it from the chart.

Degrees Magnetic: with respect to the Magnetic North Pole – if you had no ferrous objects on your vessel, this is what your compass would show due to the effect of **variation.**

Degrees Compass: this is what your compass actually reads due to **variation and deviation.**

Here are two mnemonics:

TAWC: True Add West going towards Compass

CADET: Compass Add East going towards True

IMPORTANT – always note which type of degrees you are using, be it degT, degM or degC – this will save potentially dangerous misunderstandings.

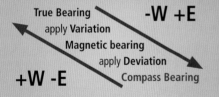

The **helmsman** always uses **degC**. It is the task of the **navigator to convert from degC and degT and vice-versa** though electronic chart plotters measure in either mode automatically

Who uses **degM**? Anyone taking bearings with a **hand-bearing compass**. Because these are not used in a fixed position on the vessel a deviation card cannot be drawn up, so take care to try and take bearings in a part of the vessel that is as ferrous-metal free as possible.

Compass heading example

It's important to have a system that you can depend on at 0230, when it's blowing hard and you're feeling seasick. Let's say you want to steer 120°T, and it's 2009 and your deviation card is as shown above.

A chart plotter takes the headache out of these compass conversions, but as with any computer, garbage in translates to garbage out. It is important to know how to calculate true and magnetic bearings manually, so that electronic aberrations stand out like a sore thumb.

True →	Variation →	Magnetic →	Deviation →	Compass
120°T	12°W	132°M	6°E	126°C

You ask the helm to steer 126°C, and the reply comes back, 'The sea state is too strong. I can only make 115°C'. You need to convert this to degT for the chart to see if this is safe and to plan around it. Use the same layout, just start from the other end – this ingrains the system.

True	← Variation	← Magnetic	← Deviation	← Compass
108° T	12° W	120° M	5° E	115° C

Assuming there is no leeway involved, this can now be plotted onto the chart and decisions made from there.

A little while later you decide to take a bearing on a lighthouse to check your progress, which is 050°M. This is done with the hand-bearing compass, and is therefore in degM. Treat this just as you did before:

True	← Variation	← Magnetic	← Deviation	← Compass
038° T	12° W	050° M		

And the true bearing of 038°T can now be plotted on the chart.

Checking your compass

It is easy to do an informal compass check by lining your vessel up with a known visible transit, such as a set of leading lights marking a harbour entrance. This is good to do on a regular basis, since it gives you confidence and acts as a check that no-one has done anything silly like leaving a toolbox or mobile phone next to the steering compass.

In this example, the bearing of the leading marks is 305°T, which is measured directly from

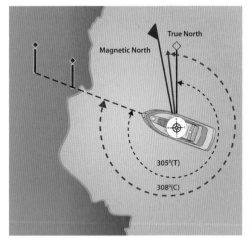

the chart. The compass heading is 308°C, which is read directly off the steering compass when the vessel is heading down the transit, and the variation is 12°W, calculated from the relevant compass rose on the chart. Following the previous example, all this is entered in the log.

True →	Variation →	Magnetic →	Deviation →	Compass
305°T	12° W	317° M	9° E	308° C

The deviation is the difference between degM and degC for that heading, in this case: 317°M – 308°C = 9°E of deviation.

Comparing this to the deviation card, it should be about 6°W for this heading.

Position fixing

To be a successful navigator, you have to be able to answer these two questions at all times: 'Where are we?' 'Where are we going?' and compare this to where you have been.

Fixes in general

A fix is a position on a chart 'fixed' by the intersection of two or more **position lines** which, as the name implies, means that you are somewhere on that line. The angle at which position lines intersect is called the **angle of cut**.

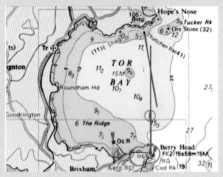

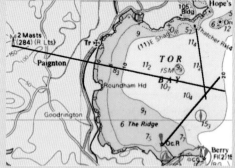

By taking bearings on *Thatcher Rock* and *Berry Head* the navigator has made a very poor fix, as the angle of cut is nearly 180° and so just a couple of degrees error (easy on a small moving boat) gives a large uncertainty (shown by the hashed area).

This gives a much better angle of cut between the two position lines, and by adding the third position line, accuracy improves further.

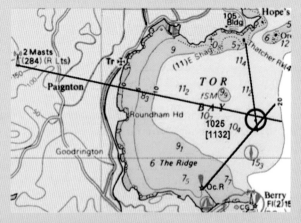

The **fix itself** is plotted as a circle with a point in the middle for the position, and every **fix** must have a **time** and a **log reading** next to it. The log reading is in brackets to differentiate between it and the time – in this example the two could easily be confused. You should estimate the fix point closest to any dangers in your 'cocked hat' (the intersection of the various position lines). This plays it as safe as possible.

Satellite navigation system fixes

GPS satellite navigation systems are now an intergrated part of navigation. They must be looked at intelligently, since with all systems that depend on software algorithms they are only as good as the data put in. Here are a few things to watch for in your system set-up:

Chart Datum: your GPS datum should be the same datum as that of the chart you are plotting the positions on.

Measurement units: check that your GPS is set to read out in nautical miles, knots and degrees true – these are all options.

Power supply: if hand-held, make sure you have enough batteries for the trip!

Aerial setup: make sure this is as per the manufacturer's recommendations and that the cable, if there is one, is secure. GPS signal problems often arise from a poorly fitted or deteriorating cable / aerial combination.

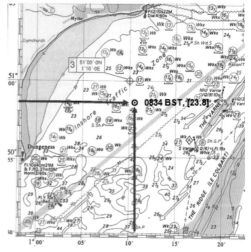

Once your plotter is set up correctly, you can take the latitude and longitude and plot these directly onto the chart. In this example the GPS position is 50°58.6'N, 001°10.7'E.

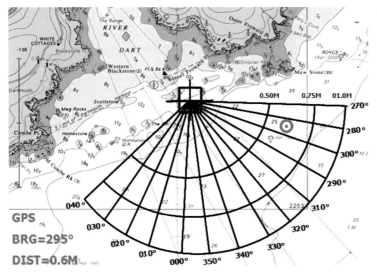

Waypoint web

This is a little time-consuming to draw up, but is excellent for high-speed navigation.

By drawing the web relative to a waypoint that the GPS is programmed to, you have a very quick way of plotting your position.

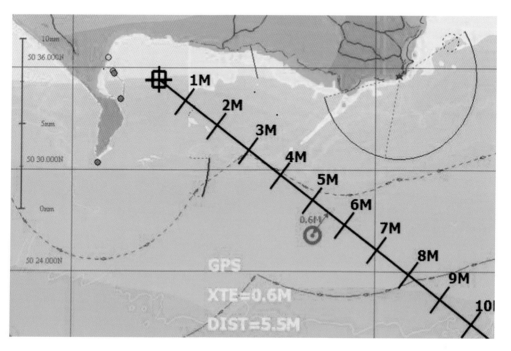

Cross track error ladder

Input two waypoints, and plot your position by distance to the destination waypoint, and XTE off the ideal track.

Electronic pilotage techniques

Clearing bearings

The clearing bearing of 255°T on the waypoint keeps you safe from the Mew Stone and other inshore rocks. Just so long as the Bearing To Waypoint is greater than 255°T, you are south of the line and therefore safe.

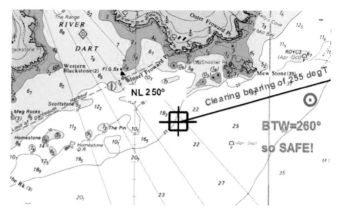

Distance off

By making a hazard into a waypoint and monitoring your distance to that waypoint, you can easily keep a safe distance off.

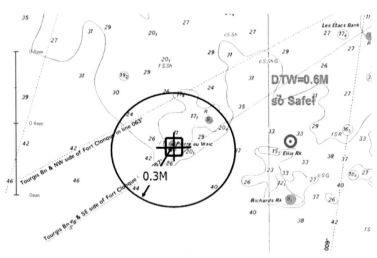

Cross track error

By setting 'no go' limits either side of the ideal track, you can use XTE to check you're not being swept to one side.

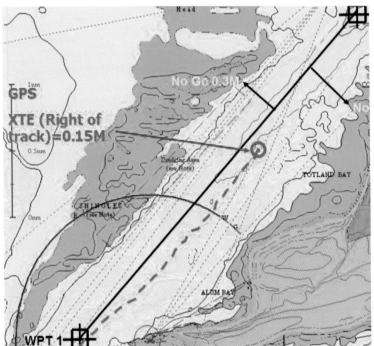

GPS for passage navigation

It is extremely important to make sure that all the waypoints are entered correctly, as a typo can have serious consequences. The major ones (50°S instead of 50°N) are fairly obvious, when you get a distance to waypoint of 12,000 nautical miles and you're only going on a weekend trip you'll notice it, but the relatively small errors that give you errors in heading of 15–20° are far more sneaky.

When planning a passage, the latitude and longitude for each waypoint has to be input with complete accuracy. The best way to check this is to compare the distance and bearings between waypoints, as calculated by the GPS, to those that you measured when you initially planned them on the chart. If all is well, they will correspond to a few tenths of a mile and a couple of degrees either way – if not, then check the waypoints on the GPS!

Visual fixes

These are taken using a combination of compass bearings, transits and depth soundings. Before going into detail, it is worth looking at what objects make good references or not.

Prominent fixed markers such as lighthouses, lit posts, church spires and headlands make excellent markers, as they do not move and are easily identifiable.

Major navigational buoys such as cardinal markers and lateral marks in busy commercial channels are also good, since they are unlikely to move. In areas of high tidal range be more careful, as their mooring chains allow significant sideways drift at low water.

Minor navigational markers such as yellow racing buoys and small lateral markers may be incorrect, their lights may not be working, or they may just not be there at all.

> **Also, do ensure your charts are up to date!**

Three-point fixes

In the following example, you have taken a series of bearings with your hand-held, magnetic compass:

Radio Mast: 270°M; Water Tower 350°M; Church Spire 050°M.

Variation is calculated as 3°W.

Convert these to degT to go on a chart. Remember the mnemonics, *TAWC* or *CADET* to decide whether to add or subtract variation.

True	← Variation	← Magnetic	← Deviation	← Compass
267°T	3°W	270°M	-	-
347°T	3°W	350°M	-	-
047°T	3°W	050°M	-	-

Unless conditions are perfect you will get a 'cocked hat' which effectively defines the potential error of the fix. It is prudent to put the fix closest to the nearest point of danger. Taking three bearings gives you much better control of visual inaccuracies.

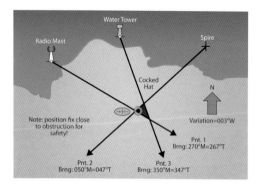

Transit fixes

These can be very useful. A transit is a line passing through two fixed objects, such as a set of leading lights, one set up behind another, as shown above by the markers leading into Nantucket. When these line up, and the **rear one** is **always highest,** you are on the transit, and this will be marked on the chart.

Equally useful are 'natural' transits, i.e. two specific charted objects coming in line so that you can draw the transit on the chart. These can be two headlands in line, or a church spire coming in line with a fixed post.

In the example, at 1542BST with a log reading of 45.8 miles, the lighthouse at *Le Stiff* lines up with the large beacon *Men Korn* to give a natural transit as a position line. There is no need to take bearings if you are sure of the identity of the two objects; all you need to

do is draw a line on the chart going through both of them. **At the same time** you take a bearing of 188°M on the large beacon *Les Trois Pierres*. Variation has previously been calculated as 7°W.

True	← Variation	← Magnetic	← Deviation	← Compass
181°T	7°W	188°M		

This can be plotted as shown and, as with every fix, the time and log reading is written on the chart.

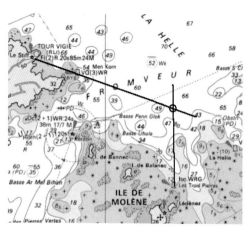

Using depth contours

Position lines don't have to be straight lines; they just have to be lines from which to check your position. Depth contours will often do for this. From a seamanship point of view, avoid using contours that pass near isolated rocks or are part of a steeply shoaling section, as this will give you very little margin for error. Looking at Tor Bay, the 10m contour in the southern and western parts of the bay is ideal, but along the north shore it gets very close to several rocks and an area of uncertain survey (dotted contour) so is unsuitable for safe navigation there.

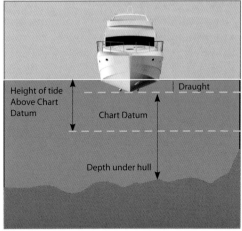

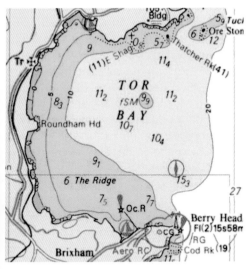

Assuming that the echo sounder is set to read zero at the bottom of the keel or rudders, then the calculation of the depth on a certain contour is as follows:
Work out the height of tide, and then:
Actual Water Depth for contour =
Contour Depth + Height of Tide
Echo sounder reading for contour =
Actual Water Depth – Draught

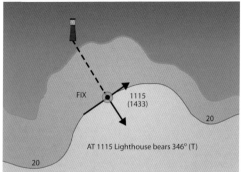

This example shows how a contour can be combined with a bearing to give a reasonable fix.

This technique does require you to know two things – the height of tide and the offset on your echo sounder. Many people like to set this so that the depth reads zero just as the hull touches bottom – this is entirely sensible, but does mean that you cannot read the water depth directly from the echo sounder.

Radar range fixes

If you have radar, this provides another way of position fixing that can be faster and more accurate than 3-point visual fixes. Small boat radars are excellent for measuring range, but poor at measuring bearing. Also, radar ranges require identifiable features, so headlands with distinctive shapes and sheer cliffs are ideal – gradually sloping beaches are not, as they don't reflect the radar signal with any definition.

A simple method is to measure the range to a feature with radar, and then use your hand-bearing compass to take a bearing. Convert this to degrees True and you can plot this bearing, measure off the distance from the radar feature using a set of drawing compasses, and where they intersect is your fix.

The example here shows a radar range off the steep cliffs of Berry Head, and a **compass bearing** of the light at the end of the breakwater. This is another example of a position line not being a straight line.

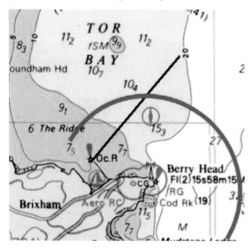

The wise navigator will use a range of navigations aids including a GPS plotter, depth sounder, compass as well as radar to plot a fix and track their course. A sister companion, *Essential Boat Radar* by Bill Johnson, provides a comprehensive overview.

Tidal flow calculation

Tidal stream atlases

These are the most visually obvious sources of tidal flow data, and are good sources for most situations, showing eddies and counter-currents well. Each tidal stream atlas covers a specific area, for example Admiralty Publication NP264, The Channel Islands and Adjacent Coasts of France. This has a separate page for each hour of tide, going from 6 hours before High Water to 6 hours after High Water. The High Water reference is that of Dover. It is important to **carefully check which port is the reference port,** as it differs for each atlas and may not even be on the area covered by the atlas, as in this case.

If we wanted to see what the tide was doing in the Little Russel between Guernsey and Herm after 0900 UT on Saturday, 7 February 2009, for example, we first need to see where we are in relation to HW Dover. The tidal data for Dover on this day is:

Dover Sat 7 Feb 2009			
	LW	0342 UT	1.69m
	HW	0855 UT	5.91m
	LW	1624 UT	1.51m

Starting at the HW page, write (in pencil) the time of HW Dover at the top, as shown.

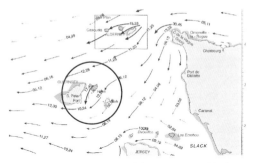

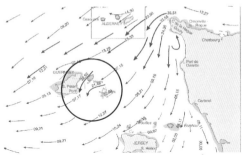

This page is valid from 30 minutes before HW Dover to 30 minutes after, i.e. 0825 to 0925UT. Alongside, the 1 hour AFTER HW Dover page, write HW Dover + 1, and carry on with this until the overall time for the planned journey is done.

This page is now valid from 0925 until 1025, when the 2 hours AFTER HW Dover page starts. In the Little Russel at 0900, therefore, the tide is represented by an arrow. The numbers represent the rates in tenths of a knot at Mean Neap and Mean Spring tides respectively, i.e. 1.7 knots at neaps, 4.0 knots at springs.

At the front of each tidal stream atlas and in each local almanac is a Computation of Rates table, which allows you to work out tidal flow rates when you're not exactly at springs or neaps. The basic principle behind this is that the greater the RANGE of tide that day (up the vertical axis), the greater the RATE will be (along the horizontal axis), as there is more water to flow in and out in the same time between high and low water. At Dover in the morning of Saturday, February 7, 2009 the range of tide is **Range = HW − LW = 5.91m − 1.51m = 4.4m**

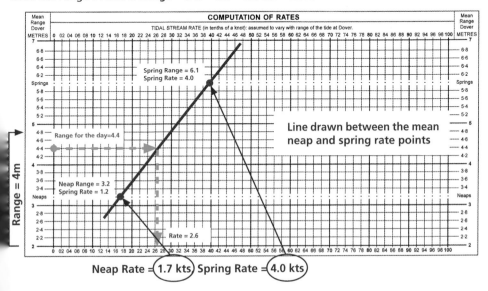

Do extend the line past the neap and spring lines – these are MEAN values, and if you have a high spring or a low neap you will need to go above or below the lines.

The interpolated **rate** is therefore 2.6 knots, and the **direction** is taken directly from the arrow. Remember – this is **only valid for the hour covered by each page**, and you need to be on the right page for the right time.

These are another representation of tidal data, designated on the charts as magenta diamonds, to provide the tidal stream data at a particular point.

Tidal diamonds

This example is from Admiralty Chart Number 5606.1, Southern North Sea and Dover Strait. The reference port is DOVER. Each column is a particular diamond, and gives its latitude and longitude – for example 50° 56.2'N, 1° 16.7' for diamond A.

TIDAL INFORMATION

5606·1 Tidal Streams referred to HW at DOVER

Hours	Geographical Position	◇A 50°56'2 N 1 16·7 E			◇B 50°59'9 N 1 34·0 E			◇C 51°26'0 N 1 38·9 E			◇D 51 1	
	Directions of streams (degrees) / Rates at spring tides (knots) / Rates at neap tides (knots)											
Before High Water 6		233	2·2	1·2	260	1·8	1·2	137	0·5	0·3	231	1
5		232	2·5	1·4	260	2·6	1·8	164	1·1	0·6	218	2
4		233	2·1	1·2	260	2·9	2·0	173	1·6	0·9	213	2
3		232	0·9	0·5	260	2·7	1·9	189	1·9	1·1	206	2
2		050	0·4	0·2	270	1·2	0·8	201	1·5	0·8	207	1
1		052	1·2	0·7	035	0·8	0·5	240	0·7	0·4	053	0
High Water		058	2·6	1·5	060	1·7	1·1	328	1·0	0·5	040	1·
After High Water 1		052	2·3	1·3	060	2·5	1·7	353	1·5	0·8	035	2·
2		052	1·8	1·0	060	2·6	1·8	004	1·6	0·9	040	2·
3		055	1·0	0·6	060	1·9	1·3	016	1·3	0·7	030	1·
4			0·0	0·0	053	0·8	0·5	026	1·0	0·5	023	1·
5		232	0·8	0·4	277	0·5	0·6	044	0·6	0·3	345	0·
6		232	1·8	1·0	260	1·9	1·3	107	0·3	0·2	246	0·

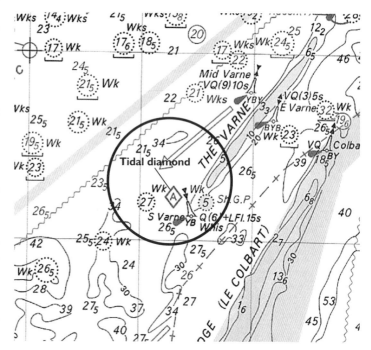

When we want to know what the tide was doing at diamond A at 0930UT on Wednesday, 11 February 2009, we need to reference this to the tide at Dover, obtained from the Almanac.

Dover Wed, 11 Feb 2009	LW 0733UT	0.46m
	HW 1218UT	6.74m
	LW 1959T	0.65m

Organisation is key, since being an hour out can completely change things. Start by seeing whether you are before or after HW. In this case, it is before.

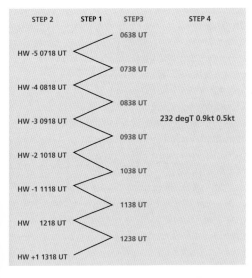

STEP 1: Make a zigzag ladder up the page, giving yourself two lines per complete zigzag.
STEP 2: Start with the HW time down towards the bottom, and write down the times of HW-1,-2,-3, etc. up the page until you are definitely past the times required.

STEP 3: On the other side of the zigzag, put the times of the start and finish of each of the tidal hours, i.e. 30 minutes before and after the hour time.
STEP 4: Look at the tidal hour start and finish times, and decide in which hour your time fits – in this case 0930UT is in the HW-3 hour, from 0838UT to 0938. The tidal diamond table shows that for diamond A at HW-3 the tide is setting at 232°T, with 0.9kts at mean springs, and 0.5kts at mean neaps.

Now all you need to do is go back to the Computation of Rates table as before (page 133) to interpolate between springs and neaps.

Logbooks, dead reckoning and estimated position – keeping track of progress

To keep a good handle on where you are, it is vital to record all the information in order to be able to reconstruct your track on the chart from your last known point, your last fix.

The logbook

The ship's log is an important legal document. Apart from navigational information, it is the place to record who you have on board and in what capacity, any standing orders, weather forecasts received, and details of any incidents; indeed anything to do with the daily running of your vessel. Navigationally, it is your primary data repository for where you've taken your vessel and what the conditions were like. Log entries should be made:

- On the hour
- When the course changes on passage
- Record radio traffic involving your vessel
- When any incident or accident occurs

- Weather reports half-hourly
- Position reports half-hourly
- Monitor engine instrument readings

If you are following the channel down an estuary, for example, it is not possible to record every course change, so there is an element of practicality involved. A recommendation would be to record the start and finish of it. For example:

1500: Started MOB drills with new crew in open water 1 mile west of harbour entrance; 1545: Finished drills. On passage now.

There are many good logbooks available. Make sure the data columns cover everything you want. The important ones are:

Navigational data

Time: Usually local time is most convenient. If you're on an ocean passage you may find it convenient to keep time in UT – this is an entirely personal choice. The important thing is to record what time you are using.

Course steered: This is what the helm has been steering **since the last log entry** – it may well be different to what the helm was asked to steer! It is important to know what has actually happened. In this case the course steered was 260°C until 1100BST when it was changed to 280°C.

Deviation & variation: Obtained from the vessel's deviation card and the chart respectively.

True course: This can be used on the chart.

Log reading: Taken directly from the vessel's instruments, ideally to the nearest cable (tenth of a nautical mile).

Position: Taken from your hourly fix, usually a GPS reading.

Weather and conditions

True wind direction: If your instruments are calibrated correctly you will be able to obtain this there, otherwise it's a case of visual observation.

True wind speed: Ideally from properly calibrated instruments, otherwise observation and experience.

Leeway: The amount your vessel is pushed sideways by the wind and or tidal stream.

Barometer: A very important weather forecasting tool. In this case it is dropping steadily. Don't tap barometers – that just puts in an incorrect offset.

Sea state: From observation.

Cloud cover: Given in oktas – coverage of the sky from one eighth to eight eighths.

Weather/visibility: By observation – are you getting wet, and if so how much? Include temperature.

These observations give an overall picture of the weather. In this case it is deteriorating, but not rapidly. By comparing it with a previous forecast and ideally a synoptic chart, you can make an informed opinion about the weather systems, and whether it is safe to continue or not.

Time	Course steered (°C)	Deviation	Variation	True Course (°T)	Log Reading	Position (GPS)
1100 BST	260° C	3° W	3° W	254°T	1106.8	Lat/long
1200 BST	280° C	6° W	3° W	271°T	1114.9	Lat/long

True Wind Direction	True Wind Speed	Leeway	Barometer	Sea State	Cloud Cover	Weather/ Visibility
200°T	20 kts	7°	1003	Moderate	6/8	Showers/moderate
220°T	22 kts	7°	1002	Moderate	8/8	Squalls/mod or poor in squalls

Vessel & voyage information

Power	Fuel	Notes
2,000	½ tank	Bouncy. Jim recovered from seasickness. Eddystone Lighthouse sighted off starboard beam, bears 355°M.
2,000	⅓ tank	Still bouncy. Jim on helm with big grin.

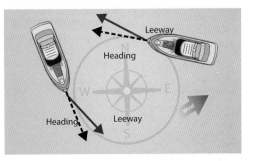

Power: Enter revs

Fuel: Monitor fuel consumption

Notes: Whatever is relevant – dolphins sighted, for example.

Leeway

Leeway is the amount that a vessel is pushed off its heading by the wind and tidal stream. Look back at your wake. The difference in direction between the line of the wake and the centreline of the vessel is the amount of leeway you have. Leeway is always put onto the TRUE heading of the vessel, and not the course heading through the water. Whether you add it on or take it off depends on the composite direction of the wind and stream. It is good to make a drawing of the situation.

In the case of the vessel (right) the heading is 280°T. The powerboat will be pushed away from the wind, so leeway (in this case say 8°) needs to be ADDED to the heading to give the true course of 288°T, which can now be plotted on the chart.

In the second example (left), the powerboat has the same SW wind beam on, and is heading 170°T. The vessel is being pushed away from the wind, so the 8° of leeway needs to be SUBTRACTED, giving a true course of 162°T which can be plotted on the chart.

A general rule:

STARBOARD SUBTRACT, PORT ADD.

Dead Reckoning (DR) – The most basic guess

This allows you to plot the vessel's position taking account of its relative movement through the water. In the example below, only the log book columns essential to this are shown.
5° leeway to port, SUBTRACT **075°T on chart**

Time	Course°C	Log	Wind	Leeway	Position	Comment
1230UT	Pilotage	102.3	SE f5	5°	0.5 M N of breakwater	Out of harbour, onto course of 080°C
1300UT	080°C	105.5	SE f5	5°	DR	Maintaining 080°C

True	← Variation	← Magnetic	← Deviation	← Compass	True →	Variation →	Magnetic →	Deviation →	Compass
080°T	3°W	083°M	3°E	080°C	305°T	12°W	317°M	9°E	308°C

Track length = Log at 1300 – log at 1230 = 3.2 nautical miles
The fix is plotted, and then the track, including leeway plotted from that initial fix. The DR is denoted by a dash across the track at the relevant point, and has the time and log reading next to it. Since this is the **water track,** it is denoted by 1 arrowhead, as shown below.

Time	Course°C	Log	Wind	Leeway	Position	Comment
1230UT	Pilotage	102.3	SE f5	5°	0.5 M N of breakwater	Out of harbour, onto course of 080°C
1300 UT	080°C	105.5	SE f5	5°	DR	Still close-hauled on starboard tack

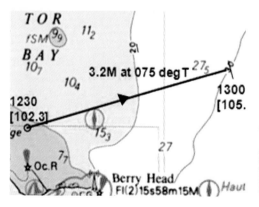

Estimated Positions (EPs)

This is the most educated estimate of the vessel's position in the water.

Effectively, an EP is a DR with tidal set and drift added on. Using the previous example of a DR:

5° leeway to port, SUBTRACT
075°T on chart

True	← Variation	← Magnetic	← Deviation	← Compass
080°T	3°W	083°M	3°E	080°C

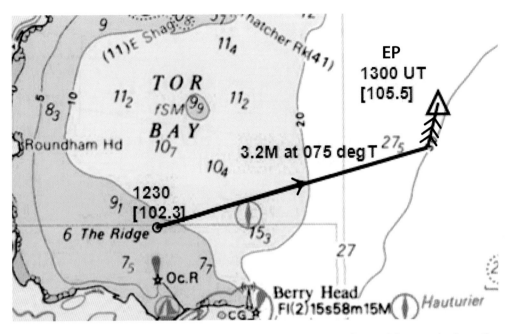

Track length = Log at 1300 − Log at 1230 = 3.2 nautical miles

Looking at the chart shows that tidal diamond B is close by. Using this as shown on page 134 you calculate that the tidal flow for this period of time, 1230UT to 1300UT is 0.5 knots towards 010°T. So to complete the EP, plot the DR as before and then add the tidal vector to it. The tidal vector is denoted by three arrow heads, and the EP is shown as a triangle.

Plotting a course to steer

So far, we have discussed where we are and where we have been. Of equal importance is where we are going, and how to allow for tide and leeway to calculate the shortest course between two places.

You are at the position marked on the chart below, and want to navigate to a position half a mile due south of Thatcher Rock to give you a safe approach into the delights of Torquay. With the current conditions the estimated boat speed will be 12 knots, with 6° of leeway, and variation is 3°W. The procedure is as follows:

1. Draw the **projected ground track** to the destination and beyond, and measure the distance to travel – in this case 6.0 nautical miles.

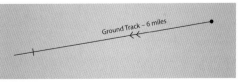

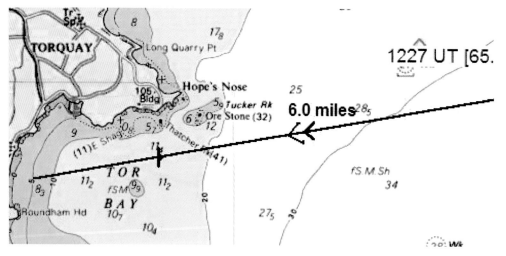

TORQUAY · Long Quarry Pt · Hope's Nose · Tucker Rk · Ore Stone (32) · TOR BAY · Roundham Hd · fS.M.Sh

1227 UT [65.

6.0 miles

2. Calculate the approximate time for the journey – it's 6 miles long and our boat speed is 12 knots, so it will take half an hour or so. This is an estimate only, and allows us to work out the period of time over which to calculate the tide.

Dover Sat 7 Feb 2009	LW	0342UT	1.69m
	HW	0855UT	5.91m
	LW	1624UT	1.51m

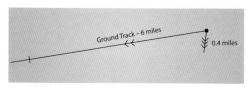

By using the method on page 148 it gives you 4 hours after HW Dover as the main part of the journey.

Now plot the tidal vector for the time period of your journey. Make it easy by using full distances. The triangle on the chart finishes before the destination. This means that it will take slightly more than 30 minutes to get to Torquay.

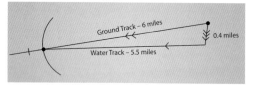

Journey times and estimated times of arrival

To estimate times, you must work with the ground track. Charts are compiled with respect to land, and your arrival and destination points are plotted likewise. So, too, must be your speed, distance and time calculations. There is one basic equation:

$$Speed = \frac{Distance}{Time}$$

This makes sense when you think about knots – nautical miles per hour, or distance over time.

To juggle these three quantities around, remember the DST triangle: Cover up the one you want, and the other two are given.

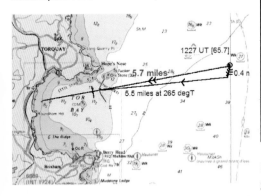

Cover up	Speed =	$\dfrac{\text{Distance}}{\text{Time}}$
Cover up	Time =	$\dfrac{\text{Distance}}{\text{Speed}}$
Cover up	Distance =	Speed x Time

Remember – everything here is with respect to the ground, so you need to use SOG – speed over ground – in all the calculations.

Referring to the previous example, the length of the ground track from the start point to the interception of the water track (the interception is shown in red) is 5.7 miles.

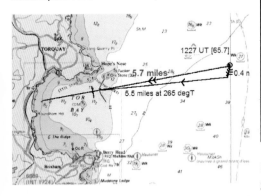

This means that the ground track is 5.7 nautical miles long over a period of 30 minutes.

Speed Over Ground

$$\text{SOG} = \text{Distance/time}$$
$$= 5.7 \text{ miles/30 minutes}$$
SOG = 11.4 knots

The distance of the journey is 6.0 nautical miles, measured in Step 1 of Course to Steer.

$$\text{Time} = \text{Distance/Speed}$$
$$\text{Time} = \frac{\text{Distance to destination}}{\text{Speed Over Ground}}$$
$$= \frac{6.0 \text{ miles}}{11.4 \text{ knots}}$$
$$= 0.525 \text{ hours}$$
$$\text{Time} = 31.5 \text{ minutes}$$

The time of the fix was 1227UT, so

Estimated Time of Arrival (ETA) = Start time + journey time

$$\text{ETA} = 1227\text{UT} + 31 \text{ minutes}$$
$$\text{ETA} = 1258\text{UT}$$

Relationship between water track and ground track

This somewhat daunting phrase sums up the relationship between the vessel's motion through the water **(water track)**, the water's motion over the ground **(tidal set, or direction – and drift, or rate)** and the boat's motion over the ground **(ground track).**

Each of these tracks is defined by a speed and a direction. These are all expressed in **knots and degrees True.**

Water track: Defined by **heading (including leeway)** and **log speed**

Tide track: Defined by **set** and **drift**

Ground track: Defined by **course over ground (COG)** and **speed over ground (SOG)**

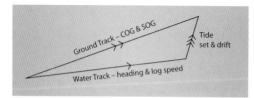

The ground track is the result of drawing the water track and adding the tide track to the end of it, just like doing an EP. It is essential that **all three tracks have the same time period.**

Water track: One arrow (1 bow wave per hull)

Ground track: Two arrows (2 footprints on the ground)

Tide track: Three arrows

Looking at the EP worked through in the previous section, the triangle can be completed as shown.

Each side of this triangle is over 30 minutes of time. The ground track is 3.5 miles long, with a bearing of 067°T. **This is the track along which the vessel has moved,** even though its course through the water was 075°T. Hence:

Course Over Ground (COG) = 067°T

As it has travelled 3.5 miles in 15 minutes, over 60 minutes it would travel 4 x 3.5 = 14 miles. 14 miles in 1 hour give a **Speed Over Ground (SOG) of 14 knots.**

The running fix

This is a useful technique for taking a visual fix while running down the coast and only one identifiable object can be seen at a time – when the weather is hazy and you only have 2–3 miles' visibility.

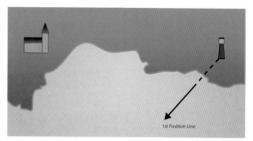

The diagram shows a visible lighthouse, with the church not yet in sight. Take a bearing on the lighthouse. After converting it to degrees True, plot that on the chart. All you know for sure is that you are somewhere on this line; you can use other data to give a better idea (for example depth), but this is the only decent bit of data you have at the time.

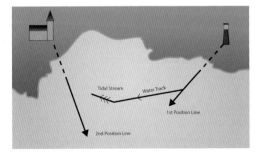

Guesstimating your position on the first position line, you continue down the coast until you can take a bearing on the church. Convert it to degrees True and plot it on the chart, as well as an EP from your guesstimated position on the first position line.

You know three things. You **were** on the first position line, you **are** on the second, and you **have moved** as defined by your EP between the two.

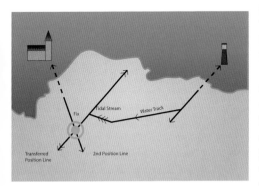

By transferring your first position line, which means taking the bearing of the first object, the lighthouse, and drawing that across the end of your EP, you will find that crosses the second position line – this is your fix!

'Where am I?' and 'Where am I going?' – The 6 minute rule

Picture the scene – it's 0245 Summer Time. You are heading up the eastern Solent, into a 10 knot westerly breeze with an ebb tide beneath you, heading for a marina in Cowes. A few miles out, one engine packs up. Not a problem, you can continue under power from the second engine, and there are plenty of mooring buoys to pick up along the way to pick if further problems are experienced.

The Solent is well lit, you know that just so long as you avoid rough water and keep a good eye out for the lights marking the Brambles Bank you won't run aground anywhere. So, apart from checking every few minutes where you are, and keeping a good lookout, you don't worry too much about the navigation. So far so good. But then, suddenly an unlit yellow racing marker whizzes by frighteningly close to the boat.

The big problem is that while you've been doing all sorts of useful things, you have only ever answered the question 'Where WAS I?',

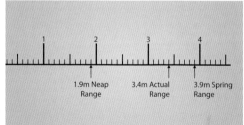

The next step is to have the tidal stream atlas (or diamonds) labelled up with the correct times. This should be done anyway prior to arriving in the area covered by the atlas. This allows you to see at a glance what the tide is doing. In this example, we see:

instead of the really important questions, 'Where AM I?' and 'Where am I GOING?'. The 6 minute rule is an easy, quick and accurate way of doing that, and after very little practice it takes seconds to use.

Why 6 minutes? It's one tenth of an hour, which makes the sums easy, especially at 0245 when conditions are rough. A bit of preparation is needed for this, so let's go through it all from the start, taking this example.

Portsmouth:

0159UTC 0259BST	4.5m	
0721UTC 0821BST	1.1m	
Range	**3.4m so 75% Springs.**	

The edge of your plotter is a good tool for working this one out. In your navigation notebook, draw a line and mark out the spring and neap ranges on it (from the Portsmouth tidal curve, in this case). The actual range is three quarters of the way from the neap range to the spring range, and an eyeball estimation will give you reasonable accuracy.

So, we can interpolate 75% of springs to be about 1.6kts, or, by using the plotter method, also about 1.6kts.

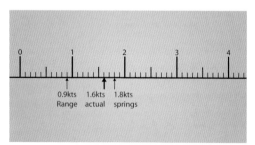

In practice an eyeball interpolation will get you to within 0.2 kts of the theoretically correct figure. This is all the preparation work you need – so far a couple of minutes at most.

You now have a line on the chart which tells you where you ARE and where you're GOING at any given time, as opposed to just a fix, which only tells you where you WERE. The beauty is that the only maths you've needed is to divide a number by 10 – with no awkward speed/time/distance calculations to be done.

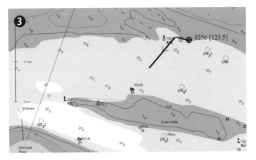

This is your starting point – a fix at 0256 BST.

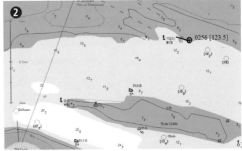

Plot one tenth of an hour, 6 minutes, worth of tide on from your fix. In this case that's 0.16 miles.

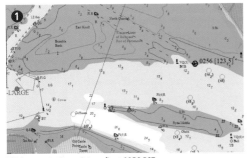

You are steering '235 on the compass at about 10 knots'. After taking into account variation, deviation and leeway, this is plotted, again using one tenth of an hour's worth of water track, i.e. 1 mile.

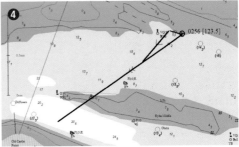

Measure the length of the ground track between your fix and the end of the water track, and walk the dividers along the ground track, marking off the notches. Each one represents 6 minutes worth of your boat's track over the ground. However, you are doing just over 12 knots of ground speed.

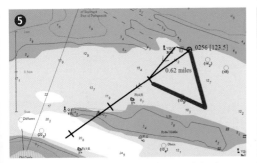

Now you can work out your ground track, by extrapolating from your fix through the end of the water track and as far out as is necessary, as shown below. This shows that you're heading for the unlit yellow racing buoy 'SL'. Now you need to know how much time you've got.

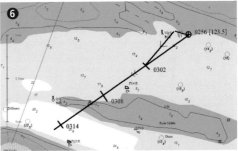

So, the last bit of chart work is to label each notch. From this, you can see, by eyeballing the ground track, that you will be abeam the Fl(4)R port-hand marker at about 0300, and getting perilously close to the unlit yellow at about 0303.

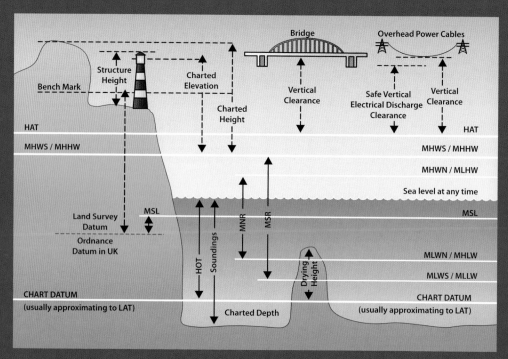

Tidal heights

In many parts of the world these are very significant, with tidal ranges (the difference between high and low water) being in the order of 15m. There are a few definitions, best illustrated by a diagram.

Chart Datum: the **vertical** datum. All drying heights and depths are referenced to this, and this is the point of zero tidal height.

LAT: Lowest Astronomical Tide. This is close to, but not necessarily equal to Chart Datum. For example, London Bridge at very low spring tides occasionally has - 0.1m of tide.

MLWS: Mean Low Water Springs, sometimes found as Mean Low Low Water (MLLW). Spring lows can be lower than this; it is a mean, or average, figure.

MLWN: Mean Low Water Neaps, sometimes found as Mean High Low Water (MHLW). This is an average; very 'neapy' neaps can have higher low waters.

Sea Level: This is Chart Datum plus the Height of tide. This is the actual water depth at any given time.

MHWN: Mean High Water Neaps, sometimes found as Mean Low High Water (MLHW).

MHWS: Mean High Water Springs, sometimes found as Mean High High Water (MHHW).

HAT: Highest Astronomical Tide.

Tide tables

Almanacs and local pilot guides give tide tables for any standard port at any day of the year. These tables give the times and heights of the low and high waters each day. As well as providing HW and LW times and heights, the tables also give information about the Moon, and whether you are at springs, neaps, or, as is more likely, somewhere in between. 9th February has a white circle next to it, signifying a full moon, and the 25th a black circle, signifying a new moon. About a day or so after these, the HW and LW marks are at their most extreme, in other words at springs. On 2nd and 16th February there is a half moon, and a day or so after, the HW and LW marks are closest together, indicating neap tides.

You will invariably need to calculate tidal heights in between HW and LW, and for that you need the tidal curve, shown below for Portsmouth. The curve shows the tide rising up from LW to a peak at HW, then falling off towards the next LW. Each tidal curve is different, and depends on the local geography and topography of the sea bed. Portsmouth is in the semi-enclosed waters of the Solent, and has quite different flow regimes for flooding and ebbing tides. Also given in the title box are the mean Spring and Neap ranges – allowing you to decide which of the curves to use, or how far in between them to interpolate.

If the range is 3.9m, then use the Springs curve for Portsmouth; if 1.9m the Neaps, and if 2.9m, draw a curve half way between.

Some ports have Low Water curves. This happens when the HW is not well defined, usually in semi-enclosed waters. Southampton is one example.

High & low water at Falmouth   FEBRUARY 2009
See inside front cover for time factors for other ports

Time	m		Time	m		Time	m		Time
1 0242	1.3		**9** 0448	5.4		**17** 0410	1.8		**25** 0526
0836	4.9		1137	0.6		0948	4.4		1210
SU 1505	1.3		M 1721	5.2		TU 1632	2.0		W 1750
2056	4.7		O 2357	0.6		2213	4.3		●
2 0318	1.5		**10** 0536	5.6		**18** 0501	2.2		**26** 0022
0915	4.8		1225	0.3		1041	4.0		0604
M 1544	1.5		TU 1809	5.4		W 1732	2.3		TH 1243
☽ 2140	4.6					2323	4.1		1826
3 0403	1.6		**11** 0042	0.4		**19** 0617	2.4		**27** 0054
1008	4.6		0624	5.7		1218	3.9		0640
TU 1636	1.8		W 1308	0.2		TH 1854	2.5		F 1313
2242	4.4		1853	5.4					1859
4 0507	1.9		**12** 0123	0.3		**20** 0120	4.1		**28** 0123
1121	4.3		0707	5.7		0751	2.4		0713
W 1752	2.0		TH 1347	0.3		F 1407	4.0		SA 1343
			1932	5.3		2035	2.3		1929
5 0004	4.3		**13** 0200	0.5		**21** 0234	4.3		
0645	2.1		0745	5.5		0927	2.0		
TH 1250	4.3		F 1423	0.5		SA 1506	4.3		
1936	2.0		2005	5.2		2148	1.9		
6 0135	4.4		**14** 0233	0.7		**22** 0325	4.6		
0828	1.9		0818	5.3		1018	1.6		
F 1420	4.4		SA 1454	0.9		SU 1553	4.6		
2104	1.7		2033	5.0		2234	1.5		
7 0253	4.7		**15** 0304	1.1		**23** 0409	4.9		
0945	1.5		0844	5.0		1058	1.3		
SA 1533	4.7		SU 1524	1.3		M 1634	4.8		
2212	1.4		2058	4.8		2313	1.3		
8 0356	5.1		**16** 0335	1.5		**24** 0448	5.1		
1046	1.0		0912	4.7		1135	1.1		
SU 1631	5.0		M 1554	1.6		TU 1711	4.9		
2308	0.9		☾ 2129	4.5		2349	1.1		

All times are U.T.

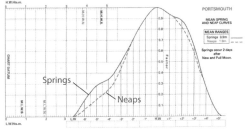

Interpolate for tides between neaps and springs.

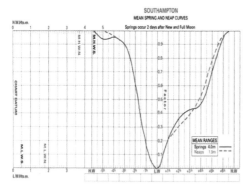

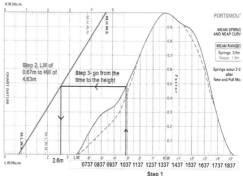

Working out the height of tide for a given time

Using Friday, 13 February 2009 as an example, the tidal data for Portsmouth is:

Portsmouth, 13 Feb 2009			
	HW	0129UT	4.75m
	LW	0649UT	0.67m
	HW	1337UT	4.63m
	LW	1907UT	0.59m

To calculate the height of tide at 1030UT:

Step 1: Fill out the time boxes, with the relevant HW as a reference. Each time written is the middle of the hour for that box, and each small subdivision is 10 minutes.

Step 2: Draw the height line from the LW value to the HW value, and note the range (in this case Range = 4.63m – 0.67m = 3.96m).

Step 3: Enter the time axis at the desired time, go up to the relevant curve, which in this case, is the Springs one since the range for the day is very close to the mean Springs range. Go across to the height line, and read off the height of tide – 2.6m

The procedure is the same when using a Low Water curve, except that you use a LW time in the centre of the time boxes. You do this when planning the time to leave a marina with a tidal sill, or you need to know the earliest you can launch your boat from its trailer in the morning.

Take the situation where you need to dry out your boat to paint her bottom in Southampton. You are able to start work once the height of tide gets below 2.5m. You need to calculate the available window.

The tide tables for Southampton give you:

13 Feb 2009			
	LW	0655UT	0.4m
	HW	1310UT	4.7m
	LW	1913UT	0.4m
14 Feb 2009			
	HW	0134UT	4.4m

For an online worldwide tide calculator visit: http://easytide.ukho.gov.uk

Using the method opposite and entering the desired 2.5m height of tide, go to the rising height curve, which is a Spring curve due to the range. The time can be read off as 2343UT

Secondary ports

If every single port had its own tide tables and curve then it would mean that you'd have to buy massive tomes of nautical almanacs to have all that data.

A way of getting round this is to designate the main ports as **standard ports**, and have all the minor ones in the area refer to their particular standard port with some corrections. These are **secondary ports.**

Secondary ports use the **same tidal curve as their standard port**, and need adjusted times and heights to make them work.

Plymouth, 13 Feb 2009:

LW	0212UT	0.5 m
HW	0812UT	5.7 m
LW	1433UT	0.6 m
HW	2032UT	5.4 m

To make the tidal curve work we need a HW time for the middle of the time axis, and a LW and HW height. It is a good idea to make a table up to remind yourself of this, as it will prevent you from converting numbers that you don't need.

	HW time	HW height	LW height (1)	LW height (2)
Standard Port	0812UT	5.7m	0.5m	0.6m
Difference				
Secondary Port				
Summer time?				

TORQUAY Standard Port PLYMOUTH							
Times				Heights in Metres			
High Water		Low Water		MHWS	MHWN	MLWN	MLWS
0100	0600	0100	0600	5.5	4.4	2.2	0.8
1300	1800	1300	1800				
+0025	+0045	+0010	0000	-0.4	-0.9	-0.4	-0.1

Each secondary port has a table in the almanac giving the required information, as shown for Torquay below.

This converts the Plymouth heights and times into Torquay heights and times. Say you want to use the tidal curve for Torquay for the morning of Friday, 13 February 2009.

As the standard port is Plymouth, write down the Plymouth tidal information.

To convert the times, look at the conversion table for high water times.

Times
High Water
0100   0600
1300   1800
_____
+0025   +0045

This means that if HW Plymouth was either 0100 or 1300, if you add 25 minutes, you get HW Torquay. Similarly, if HW Plymouth was either 0600 or 1800, you add 45 minutes to get HW Torquay.

If the HW height was exactly 5.5m, i.e MHWS, then the correction would be -0.4 and HW Torquay at MHWS would be 5.1m. Usually interpolation is required.

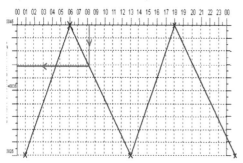

In this case, we need only to convert one time, 0812UT. That is shown in the diagram above, and gives a correction of +0039 minutes, and a HW Torquay of 0851UT.

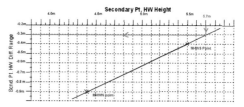

In this example, the standard port HW height is above the MHWS mark, so the line between the MHWS and MHWN points must be extended. This gives a correction of -0.3m.

	HW time	HW height	LW height (1)	LW height (2)
Standard Port	0812UT	5.7m	0.5m	0.6m
Difference	+0039	-0.3m		
Secondary Port	0851UT	5.4m		
Summer time?	No			

It doesn't matter which way round the axes on the graph go, or where each axis starts.

The LW heights are done in the same way. The reason that we are doing two LW heights is that the tide comes up from the previous LW to the central HW and down to the following LW, and we want to look at the tide for the entire morning. Depending on what tidal data you want, you may only have to do one HW and one LW.

	HW time	HW height	LW height (1)	LW height (2)
Standard Port	0812UT	5.7m	0.5m	0.6m
Difference	+0039			
Secondary Port	0851UT			
Summer time?	No			

The HW height is converted using a similar process.

Heights in Metres

MHWS	MHWN
5.5	4.4
-0.4	-0.9

Heights in Metres

MLWN	MLWS
2.2	0.8
-0.4	-0.1

Looking at the LW column, when the standard port LW is 2.2m, i.e MLWN, the correction is -0.4m. When it is at 0.8m, i.e MLWS, the correction is -0.1m.

As the Standard Port LW is below MLWS, the line is extended as before. This gives the final two corrections. It doesn't matter which way round the axes on the graph go, or where each axis starts.

	HW time	HW height	LW height (1)	LW height (2)
Standard Port	0812UT	5.7m	0.5m	0.6m
Difference	+0039	-0.3m	+0.1m	+0.1m
Secondary Port	0851UT	5.4m	0.6m	0.7m
Summer time?	No			

(For standard port curve see page 148)

This can now be used just as any other tidal curve. It is no longer a Plymouth curve, and therefore the Plymouth mean spring and neap ranges no longer apply.

Pilotage

This is the art of navigating from safe water outside a harbour to your berth, avoiding any dangers en route. This could be navigating into New York Harbor from the Ambrose Lighthouse, or through the Needles Channel at the western entrance of the Isle of Wight from the safe water mark there. Pilotage is also needed in the middle of passages if your route takes you through confined waters, like the Chenal du Four between Ushant and France when heading south to Bordeaux from the UK.

Pilotage is different to offshore passage navigation in that it is very visual, and depends on maintaining a course along well-defined legs with clear indicators. There is generally no time to plot pilotage on the chart, so you need all the information to hand. It can be quite time-consuming to prepare properly, but is essential for a safe entry into port, especially if conditions are tricky. It is, after all, the shallow bits at the beginning and end of a journey that do the damage – the blue water sections in the middle are generally more straightforward.

Clearing bearings

This is an excellent technique used for **staying to one side of a known danger.** Let's say you're approaching Tor Bay from the north, and want to stop in Torquay alongside the pier and use the crane to off-load some heavy gear. There are several unmarked rocks and small islands at the NE entrance to the bay.

By using two clearing bearings in succession you can stay clear of all of these with a minimum of fuss and a maximum of visual certainty.

To start with you need to avoid Tucker Rock and the Ore Stone. Draw a **clearing bearing** on the very obvious Berry Head lighthouse. By staying to the east, you will be in safe water, clearing the Ore Stone by about 4 cables, or 0.4 nautical miles. By staying east, the bearing of Berry Head will be greater than your clearing bearing. If you are to the west it will be less – and you only need to remember one number!

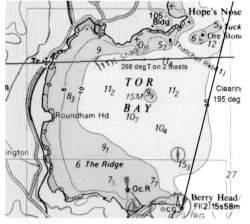

As you pass the Ore Stone, (which at 32m high should be visible even at night), start looking to the west for the two masts, 284m high, lit with red lights. Once seen, monitor their bearing until it becomes more than 268°T and head towards them. Just so long as you are south of this line, with the bearing to the masts greater than the clearing bearing of 268°T, you are in safe water to the south of the Ore Stone, Thatcher Rock and East Shag.

Use of depth contours

Depth contours can make excellent clearing lines. As in the previous example, if you stay deeper than the 20m contour while heading south past the Ore Stone, and then deeper than the 10m contour while heading west past the Ore Stone, Thatcher Rock and East Shag, you will be in safe water. It is vital that you **reduce measured depths to soundings,** i.e. take off the tide from your echo sounder reading, for this.

Approaching the port

As you head in, keeping south of the clearing bearing of 268°T on the masts, start to identify features nearer Torquay itself. The steep cliffs and headlands are quite imposing, and there is a rock arch at London Bridge that may be visible. The grand edifice of the Imperial Hotel will be easy to spot, especially at night with all the lights on, and the piers protecting the harbour itself, will become easier to see. The southern pier, Haldon Pier, has a quick green flashing light visible for 6 nautical miles, and just to the west of it is a QG flashing starboard hand marker. When this bears 327°T (or when the pier QG bears 330°T, should the buoy be difficult to see), turn towards it and start your approach. Keep an eye on its bearing, as cross-tide effects may take you one side or another, and warn the crew to keep a good lookout for unlit yellow markers , especially the two closest to the harbour just under half a cable off to port of your ideal track.

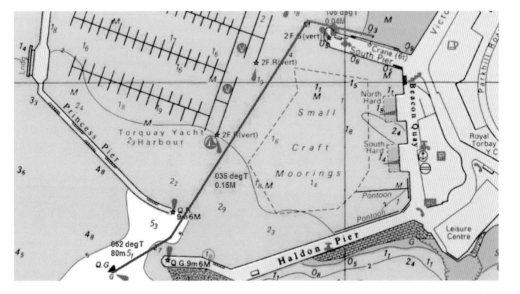

Detailed pilotage plan

This should be made on the most detailed chart you have. The crane is on the north side of South Pier, and the three legs shown will take you there. Each leg of a pilotage plan should have as a minimum four pieces of information: **start point, finish point, distance and direction.**

The start and finish points should be identifiable by eye or instrument; for example, next to a buoy, between two breakwaters or between a hammerhead pontoon and a pier end. Ideally they should be lit in case you arrive there after dark. The annotated chart (above) has all the information required for a pilotage plan, but a chart can sometimes be unwieldy on deck, especially in heavy weather. Some navigators overcome this by drawing out a separate pilotage plan, but make sure that you study the chart properly – and replicate

the hazards and landmarks correctly, to avoid potential danger and embarrassment.

Draw your track on the chart. Everything you see to port needs to be annotated on the left. Everything to starboard goes on the right. Any leg information goes in the middle.

This **starts** between the pier ends at the harbour entrance, and **finishes** on a line to the Old Fish Quay between the north end of the second hammerhead pontoon and the South Pier. The course is **0.15 nautical miles long on a heading of 035°T.** In addition, you have the first hammerhead coming up on the port side after 0.06 nautical miles, marked by 2 vertical fixed reds, and after another 0.05 miles, the second hammerhead is similarly marked. On the starboard side there are small craft moorings, so keep a lookout for unlit moored boats and tenders. There is also depth information.

Back bearings

These are very useful for keeping you on a particular bearing from a start point when tide and leeway are taking you sideways.

To make an entry into St Mawes from the flashing green starboard hand marker, you could safely do so by taking a back bearing of 240°T on it.

Keep sighting down the bearing, not directly at the buoy, since this will show you to which side of the track you have drifted. Transits also provide visual pilotage headings and clearing lines.

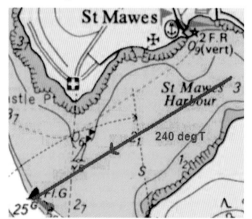

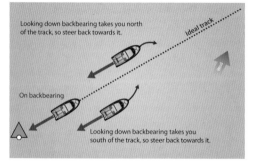

Passage planning and execution

Passage planning looks after the part of the voyage from safe water outside your point of departure to safe water outside your destination.

As the saying goes – 'no battle plan survives contact with the enemy', but with a decent passage plan you can enjoy safe, purposeful cruising and get where you originally set out to go.

There are a few basic concepts to consider:

Waypoints

These are simply points of navigational significance. In general, these are the 'corners' in your route, but you can place them anywhere you like. There is nothing wrong with using buoys as waypoints, but remember to keep a good watch when coming near – boats have a nasty habit of hitting them when running on autopilot guided by GPS!

Tidal gates

These are areas of tidal concern, such as tidal height constraint when exiting a lock or harbour entrance with a sill across it. A strong tidal flow running against a stiff wind can also cause uncomfortable or potentially dangerous sea states in certain areas.

Alternative ports

These are ports that you can plan to divert to if the weather takes a change for the worse, the vessel suffers mechanical failure or you experience other problems.

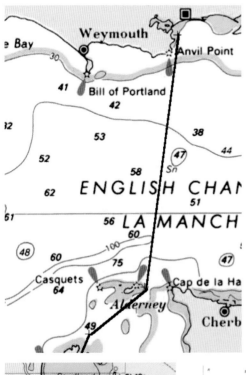

Passage planning example

You are at anchor in Studland Bay off the Dorset coast in England and planning a run to St Peter Port, on Guernsey in the Channel Islands the next day, Friday, 13 February 2009. The first step is to look at the **overall journey.**

Leg 1: This is 57 miles long, from departure cross Channel from Studland Bay to the centre of the Alderney Race. The leg starts from Waypoint 1, one nautical mile east of Old Harry, a very obvious limestone pillar.

This is a fairly arbitrary choice, and keeps you away from any shallows and overfalls until you are past Anvil Point and in open water.

From there, Leg 1 goes cross-Channel. Running your finger down the track you see there are no fixed dangers – though there will be many ships going up and down the main shipping lanes to watch out for. At the end of Leg 1, there is plenty of space coming through the Alderney Race, just so long as you are on track and have the tide right.

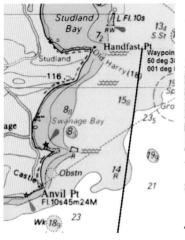

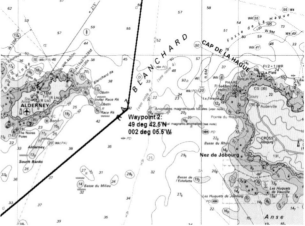

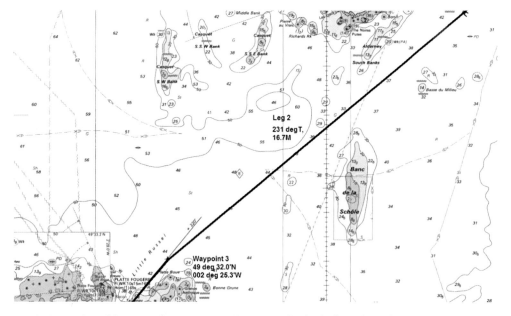

Leg 2: From the Alderney race to a waypoint on the leading lights marking the Little Russel channel to St Peter Port.

It is important to draw the track and note its heading and length **on the chart**. By running your finger along the track you check that you are not getting too close to any dangers – such as the Banc de la Schole, which is a safe distance off to the south.

This is the end of the passage plan – from Waypoint 3 to St Peter Port it is now a pilotage plan, and quite a busy and detailed one too.

Timing your passage

So far so good – you know where you're going, and you have the ideal tracks drawn on the charts that you are going to use. So, when to leave, and when to arrive?

This looks fine, though technically speaking the weather may occasionally be a bit rough, but at least the winds will be abeam or astern, so no head seas to confront.

Now look at the tides for **potential tidal gates**. There are two in this case:

- The Alderney Race, where tides can reach over 9 knots;
- St Peter Port itself, where the marina entrance has a sill with a drying height of 4.20m.

First, check the weather. The Met Office website gives the shipping forecast for UK and northern European waters *www.metoffice. gov.uk/weather/marine* The NOAA site does the same for North American waters *www. nws.noaa.gov/om/marine/home.htm* The Euroweather site covers the Mediterranean. *www.eurometeo.com/english/marine.*

Of the two, the first is more important. If you get to the marina entrance at the wrong time you can simply tie up to the waiting pontoon and put the kettle on, whereas if you get the tide wrong at the Alderney Race it will be, at best, very uncomfortable and slow, or worse – extremely dangerous.

The tidal stream atlas shows the best time to get there is just before HW Dover, when the tide is slack prior to ebbing, which will then take you all the way down to St Peter Port.

Leg 1 is 57 nautical miles long. At an average of 15 knots, this will take around 3 hours 50 minutes to complete, though it is always a good idea to allow extra time for unforeseen circumstances. This would mean weighing anchor at 1100 UT on the 13th. This would have the advantage of a later afternoon entry into St Peter Port, so this is a good option. Leg 2 is 16.7 miles long, and should take about 1 hour with the tide behind you, putting you at the entrance to the Little Russel channel at about 1600.

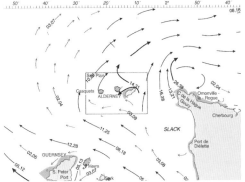
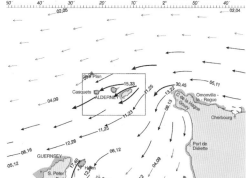

Looking at the tidal data for Dover we have:

Dover, 13th Feb 2009

HW	0112UT	6.9m
LW	0851UT	0.5m
HW	1333UT	6.5m
LW	2103UT	0.9m

14 Feb 2009

HW	0148UT	6.8m
LW	0924UT	0.8m
HW	1409UT	6.3m
LW	2103UT	1.2m

The ideal times to get to the Alderney Race are 1300UT on the 13th or 0100UT on the 14th.

The pilotage is just over 6 miles long, so, even if you slow down to 10 knots for this last section and take a further 40 minutes, sunset on the 13th is at 1726UT, so there should be reasonable light for this final part of the voyage.

You need to do a tidal curve for St Peter Port, which in this case, tells you that at 1700UT there is about 6.5m of tide, giving 2.3m over the sill. For large motor vessels, this gives only a small clearance, so you may have to wait until about 1900UT before entering the marina.

Alternative ports

On any passage you should think about the options for stopping off should the weather break or should anyone fall ill or hurt themselves.

On this passage, if something were to happen halfway across the Channel, Cherbourg would be the obvious spot – a large port with all-tide, all-weather access. However, as you close on the Alderney Race, Cherbourg becomes less attractive, since the adverse tide will be running quite strongly eastwards along the coast. So now, Braye Harbour on Alderney becomes the best option. (Consult almanac for wind effect at harbour entrance.)

This requires a pilotage plan to be made in advance just in case, coupled with a thorough study of the tides around the harbour entrance.

Calculating the overall tidal influence for an individual leg

Calculating a course to steer for a 60 mile leg is a little more involved than doing it for a trip that will only take an hour or so. One way to give yourself a good idea of the overall tidal set and drift is to look at the individual hours on your projected track. A simple table will do:

As this is over 6 hours an average tidal rate can be calculated:

$$\text{Average tide} = 1.7\text{M}/6 \text{ hours} = 0.15\text{kts to the East.}$$

This can then be put into a standard Course to Steer triangle.

Hour	West Going	East Going
1	0.4	-
2	1.5	-
3	3.0	-
4	3.3	-
5	2.6	-
6	1.9	-
7	0.4	0.8
8	0.4	2.0
9	0.4	3.9
10	0.4	3.9
11	0.4	3.2
12	0.4	0.6
Totals	12.7 M west	14.4 M east
Overall	1.7 M east	-

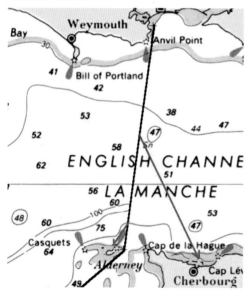

In practice, it is unlikely that this will work out exactly for several reasons, so it is a good idea to re-do your EP whenever the distance to the end of the leg reduces by half: for this passage, after 30 miles, then 45, and then whenever you feel a need to recheck.

What happens over the ground during a 12 hour period is that you will be taken nearly 13 miles west of your plotted track, and then brought back just over 14 miles by the east-going flood tide. This may look alarming as you plot your hourly positions within the time frame of your passage, but by keeping a good track of where you are in relation to the tide you should see yourself slide back to where you should be.

One way of keeping on top of things is to do a **predictive EP** on every hourly fix. Put your fix on the chart, then do an EP using your average speed and heading, together with whatever the tide is predicted to be for the next hour. In an hour's time, your next fix should be pretty close to the predicted EP. If not, it's a good sign that things are not as they should be.

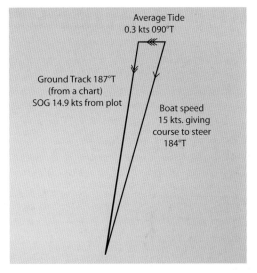

Average Tide
0.3 kts 090°T

Ground Track 187°T
(from a chart)
SOG 14.9 kts from plot

Boat speed
15 kts. giving
course to steer
184°T

Navigation tip

SHAPE – a passage
MONITOR – as you go
ADJUST – to the changing conditions

Radio etiquette

Every vessel fitted with a radio transmitter is required to have a Ship Radio Licence, and from this comes the vessel's unique call sign. This is made up of letters and numbers and is spelt out using the phonetic alphabet.

If your vessel has only a hand-held VHF set, a Ship Portable Radio Licence is required. The radio transmitter can only be operated by a ship's radio licence holder with a Short Range Certificate, or crew member under their control.

The latest digital VHF sets operate on the Global Maritime Distress and Safety System (GMDSS). This was introduced to ensure that a vessel can transmit a distress alert automatically. When connected to a GPS receiver, the system will also send your position with a distress alert.

Using a VHF radio

❶ Press to talk (PTT) microphone. Press the PTT button and the set switches from receive to transmit. Hold the microphone 2inches (5cm) from your mouth and speak slowly and clearly. Say 'Over' at the end of the message and release the PTT button.

❷ Scan. This allows the set to monitor several channels at one time.

❸ DW (Dual Watch). This allows the set to monitor priority channel 16 and one other channel.

❹ High/low power. Use low power for all routine calls

❺ Squelch. A filter to reduce background noise. Adjust knob until interference noise is just audible.

Distress button

This is on VHF-DSC sets only and is protected by a cover. The set has to be programmed with the name and type of the vessel. For a Mayday call, open the cover and press the button. Then press it again for 5 seconds. The alert will then be retransmitted every 4 minutes until a Coastguard station or other vessel responds. The nature of the distress can be defined by scrolling down the menu. NEVER test the DSC by initiating a distress alert.

Phonetic alphabet

Use the phonetic alphabet to spell out boat names, call signs, abbreviations and words

A	ALPHA	N	NOVEMBER
B	BRAVO	O	OSCAR
C	CHARLIE	P	PAPA
D	DELTA	Q	QUEBEC
E	ECHO	R	ROMEO
F	FOXTROT	S	SIERRA
G	GOLF	T	TANGO
H	HOTEL	U	UNIFORM
I	INDIA	V	VICTOR
J	JULIET	W	WHISKEY
K	KILO	X	X-RAY
L	LIMA	Y	YANKEE
M	MIKE	Z	ZULU

Over: I have finished talking and require an answer.

Out: I have finished talking and do not require an answer. Never finish a conversation with 'Over and Out', as it will lead to much ridicule and cost you a round of drinks.

Say Again: Repeat what you have just said.

Correction: An error has been made; the corrected version is to follow.

I Say Again: I am repeating my previous information.

VHF channel allocation

16: primary distress working channel, and general call-up channel

13: primary inter-bridge channel for matters relating to collision avoidance

06, 08, 72 and 77: main intership channels

70: digital signal for DSC traffic

Testing your VHF

Coastguard stations are quite happy to receive test calls, but do bear in mind that in busy waters, should 324 boats call in on Channel 16 all requesting a radio check, this important distress channel will become clogged. So, look up the Routine Traffic channel for the Coastguard in the local almanac and make your radio check call on that instead.

Calling other vessels

The VHF radio is a convenient and free means of communication but, as with the radio check calls, you don't want to hog Channel 16 discussing where to have dinner that night. So, when calling up another vessel, once you have made contact on 16, move to an intership channel.

Passage planning

Once onboard, the crew will be keen to set out. Don't be rushed into planning the voyage and setting up the nav aids. Better still, do it at home and give yourself time to double check tidal information, fuel estimates and waypoints. Then it is just a case of adding the waypoints into the GPS and making a last check on the weather forecast.

From 2010, it will be necessary in European waters at least to file a crew list and route plan each time you set out to sea, so do this ahead of time and make sure that you carry passport/ID and sailing/radio qualification certificates along with your insurance documents and ship's registration papers. Where to go? Decide on a final destination and ETA, then work back to pick rendevous or refuelling points, danger points and tidal gates, and refuge ports in the event of adverse weather or injury.

Departure port
- Passage plan

Destination port
- High and Low water times
- Depth restrictions over entrance bar or sill
- Local dangers – rocks, wrecks etc.
- Marina or harbour radio channel + telephone numbers
- Check shipping movements
- Pilotage plan to get into port.

Mooring
- Pre-book marina berth or visitors mooring
- Check anchorage – ground type, space and ferry arrangements.

List of destinations
- Distances between ports or waypoints
- Estimate passage time between points taking account of tidal stream
- Plot waypoints, traffic separation schemes, danger points and landmarks

- Estimate fuel consumption and add 20% safety margin.

Weather forecasts
- Listen to weather forecasts for 2–3 days beforehand and monitor depressions.

Food
- Plan menus and prepare food ahead of time
- Drinks – carry a minimum of 2 litres of water per person per day.

What to carry onboard
Charts of cruising area
- Almanac
- Tidal atlas
- Cruising guide
- Dividers
- Course plotter
- Pencils
- Eraser
- Pilot books.

Once onboard
- Enter waypoints into GPS course plotter
- Check latest weather forecast
- Decide go or no-go

- Check fuel and oil levels
- Crew safety briefing.

During passage
- Monitor speed, course, position and timings against passage plan
- Check fuel consumption
- Monitor engine instrument read-outs in ship's log.
- Log weather and sea state and note any changes
- Crew – keep them informed and involved.

Fall back plan decision points
- Delays
- Weather change
- Tidal gates
- Crew issues

On arrival
- Radio, or call ahead to marina or harbour office and Customs
- Raise courtesy/Q flags
- Locate mooring, berth or anchorage
- Complete passage plan documentation and log.

Navigating in restricted visibility

Fog can form at the most inopportune moments – usually when you are closing in on your intended destination! Fog often results from cold rain falling on a warmer sea surface.

Humid air on a clear night can also lead to what is termed 'radiation fog'. This is more common in the autumn months, when the nights get longer, and the water surface, still warm from the summer, evaporates. Another form is 'advection fog' which can form in the winter/spring months when a warm moist air mass blows over cold surface waters. What to do if caught in fog or poor visibility:

Preparation

- Plot a fix or EP on chart before entering fog
- Reduce speed to anticipate another vessel suddenly looming out of the fog
- Switch navigation lights on
- Set up radar reflector
- Post lookouts on flybridge and at radar
- Wear lifejackets and have liferaft ready to launch
- Sound the fog horn at regular intervals or whenever another vessel is heard
- Stop and turn off engines occasionally to listen
- If close to shipping lanes, call up the port VTS and pilotage services and give your position

- If you have any concerns call the Coastguard on Channel 16
- Proceed with caution
- Head for shallow water
- Monitor the depth
- Plot EPs, GPS fixes and soundings every 15 minutes or less
- If in shallow water consider anchoring, but remember everyone else will be heading for shallow water or navigation marks too!

Contouring

If you know your start position, well and good. If you have only an EP, then motor slowly towards the nearest contour line on your chart and monitor depth.

Use ALL available nav aids:

- Radar
- GPS
- Web from Compass Rose
- Web Ladder
- Regular waypoints
- Regular Fixes
- Route Plotter
- Head towards marks to confirm position.

Speed and distance:
Maintain a constant speed and work to the
6 Minute Rule. In six minutes, a vessel making:
- 5 knots will travel 0.5 of a nautical mile
- 10 knots will travel 1 nautical mile
- 15 knots will travel 1.5 nautical miles
- 20 knots will travel 2 nautical miles

Boat handling in heavy weather

Bad weather is a fact of life, but one big advantage that fast power cruisers have over slower vessels, is the ability to outrun the weather. The key to making a safe passage in uncertain conditions is planning and preparation.

- Check the forecasts each day
- Assess your skills, those of your crew and your powerboat, and set limits on what you determine to be safe conditions – and stay in port if they are exceeded.
- Pre-plan navigation and pilotage and include refuge ports in the passage plan to take account of an adverse change in the weather.
- Secure for sea. Stow all gear on deck and below, secure hatches and pre-prepare food for the voyage.
- Prepare the crew. Brief them on the course and expected conditions, take seasickness medication well ahead of the voyage, have a hot meal before you set out and kit everyone out with foul weather gear and life jackets.
- Set up rope lines as handholds across open areas like the cockpit.
- No access forward of the flybridge.

Stability

Most powerboats are remarkably stable thanks to their design and the relationship between their centre of gravity (CG), which needs to be kept as low as possible, and the vessel's inherent centre of buoyancy (CB).

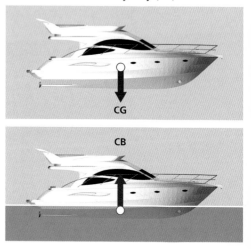

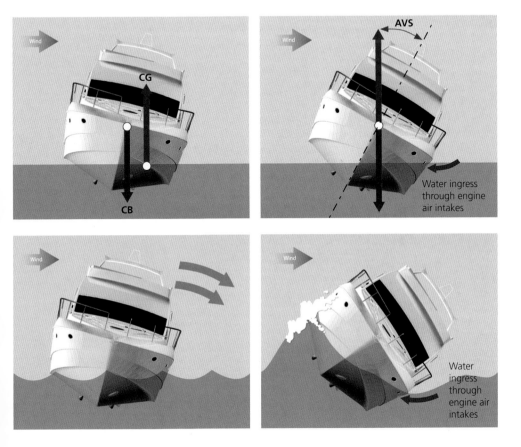

When a powerboat lists to one side, its centre of gravity and centre of buoyancy both traverse sideways towards the list. Provided the CG moves sideways faster than the CB, then the boat remains stable and will return to an even keel on its own account. But once CG overtakes the CB, the boat loses its inherent stability and has the potential to roll over. This point of no return is called the angle of vanishing stability (AVS).

In reality, this critical point is between 35–40° and can result from broaching out of control when running down waves or when caught in heavy beam seas. Additional top weight like an overcrowded flybridge as well as accessories like radar, liferaft and the addition of a fridge on the top deck all have an effect on raising the centre of gravity. Once this 35–40° angle of heel is exceeded, water ingress through air intakes and scuppers simply adds to this instability.

Heavy weather tips

- Minimise top weight by limiting crew numbers on the flybridge
- Stow heavy items like the life raft in the cockpit (but not inside the boat)
- Avoid overloading or poor trim
- Check all hatches and windows are closed and secure and cockpit drains are not blocked before setting out
- Ensure that bilge pumps work effectively – bilge water slopping from one side to another, greatly affects stability
- Avoid tidal races and over falls, breaking waves and broaching.

Adjusting outdrive trim and or trim tabs can have a considerable effect in smoothing the ride of power cruisers in heavy seas.

Tab down when running into head seas has the effect of pushing the bow downwards and will lessen slamming.

Tab up when running with the waves will stop the bows from burying itself when the stern is picked up by a following wave.

Trim tabs are sensitive enough to steer by when at speed.

Tab the starboard trim tab down and the boat will pull to starboard, and the opposite will apply when trimming the port trim tab.

They can also be used to compensate against the effects of a beam sea or strong crosswinds.

Tab one side down will raise that side of the boat and correct the list.

Tip

1. Trim down raises the stern and lowers the bow
2. Trim up raises the bow and lowers the stern

Tactics in large waves
Heading downwind

If you have the sea room, it is far better to run with the waves and head for a refuge port rather than go against them. You also have the advantage of staying ahead of worsening weather.

The one danger to avoid is a breaking wave overtaking the powerboat that catches the stern and slews the boat side-on into a broach to be at the mercy of the next wave.

The best way to avoid a broach is to match the speed to that of the waves or indeed exceed them.

❶ As the boat climbs the wave ahead, trim the bow up by raising the trim tabs or outboard/ outdrive leg and increase the throttles to match the speed of the wave.

2 As the crest breaks, ease the throttles back to reduce power as the boat accelerates naturally down the face of the wave. Ride the wave in this attitude for as long as possible.

3 Try to steer towards flatter waves or breaks in the wave patterns.

4 Keep a good lookout behind for breaking seas catching you unawares.

5 Beware of burying the bows into the wave ahead. Play the throttles and reduce speed as the boat glides down the wave, then accelerate to position the boat to ride the crest of the next wave.

Into head seas

Minimise slamming into the head seas by cutting back the throttles as the bows rise up the wave and by trimming down the tabs or outboard/outdrive legs.

Damage limitation

Windows are particularly vulnerable to being smashed by the force of the waves. Turn the boat to put the damage on the leeward side and plug the window with berth cushions and cupboard doors. If one window has been broken, others may also fail. If there is sea room, turn downwind or head for shelter. Inform the Coastguard and keep them informed of progress and when you reach safety.

❶ Wind against tide situations produce short, sharp seas. Avoid tidal races and over falls altogether, and where possible, steer a course where the tidal stream is minimal – divert around the outskirts of a bay rather than trying to head straight across, or head for shallower water if the waves are less.

2 If forced to head directly into the seas, take a zigzag course 30-40° to the waves, picking a route to avoid the breaking crests. This gives you more lead-time between waves and better chance to spot the bigger waves ahead – and avoid them.

3 If winds are above force 6, small and medium sized vessels should head for a safe haven. The risk of encountering strong wind-against-tide situations can be minimised by safe passage planning.

Towing

Commercial tugs and workboats have a stanchion post or other form of strong point to tow from. Few private vessels have the same facility, so beware of connecting a tow rope to bow or stern cleats – the tow line will simply pull them off!

Strong bridles attached to as many thru-bolted strong points as possible need to be set up on both the tug and the towed vessel. Use a long anchor line or rope of similar strength strung between the two as the tow line, tied off with bowlines to the bridles at each end.

Tug

- Keep a safe distance between you and the tow. A wave can easily surge the stricken vessel up onto your transom.
- Beware of loose lines fouling your props.

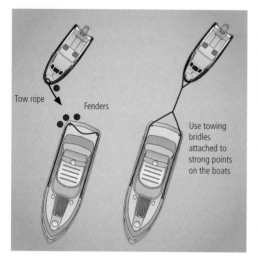

Tow rope

Fenders

Use towing bridles attached to strong points on the boats

- Check the tow attachment points on the tow vessel. If they pull out during the tow, the rope will whiplash back and damage your boat or injure your crew.
- If necessary, use a light throwing line to connect the two vessels and use this to pull the heavier tow line across.
- Keep crew out of the direct line of the tow rope.
- Start the tow downwind to minimise the acceleration forces on the rope, then turn on to the correct course once momentum has built up.

Towed vessel

Towing is a salvageable act. Agree a fee with the tug before lines are attached and log any arrangement.

- Set up a tow bridle to strong points around the boat and feed it through the bow fairleads to minimise chafe.
- If the tow vessel is much lighter than the tug and surges forward down the waves at a faster speed , deploy a bucket drogue or drag a long loop of rope astern to slow you down.
- If the rescue services come to your aid, remember that their prime concern and

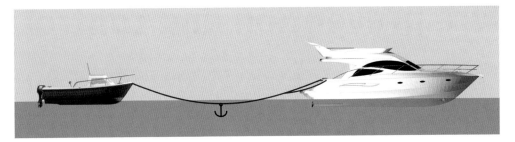

responsibility is to save lives, not property. If conditions are favourable, a lifeboat crew may be prepared to take your vessel in tow but they are not obliged to do so.

Towing
The tow line needs to be as long as possible to minimise the snatch forces.

- If possible, make the tow line long enough so that both vessels are in sync with the waves.
- If necessary, tie a heavy weight to the middle of the line to keep the line in tension and lessen the shock loadings.
- Keep speed to a minimum. The faster you go, the greater the loadings will be on tow rope and fastenings.

Standby
If the tow rope or equipment on either vessel is not strong enough, then it is far better to stand by at a safe distance to provide assistance and moral support until the professional services can reach the scene, rather than attempt a tow that could put both vessels in jeopardy.

If the need arises to evacuate the stricken crew, then position your boat at a safe distance upwind and float a dinghy or liferaft on the end of a tow line down to the stricken vessel and pull the crew across one at a time.

In harbour
In restricted waters, towing alongside gives much greater manoeuvrability.

- Fender both boats well.
- Position the tow slightly ahead with the bows pointing in of the tug in order to steer a straight line.
- Connect bow, stern and spring lines with equal tension.
- Keep speed to a minimum.

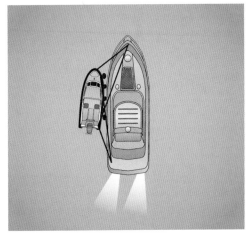

Fire prevention and control

Short of sinking, there is nothing worse than a fire onboard. Not all fires are preventable, but most are, so time spent drawing up a risk assessment and installing prevention measures may not only save your boat – but lives too.

Galley

Most boat fires start in the galley, and alcohol stoves are the worst culprits. If you have one, change it for a gas-fired cooker/stove.

- Ensure that gas canisters are stored in a locker that drains outboard of the boat, and not into the bilge
- Fit a gas detection system in the bilge and replace sensors if they get wet
- Shut off gas valve near cooker after use
- Shut off gas bottle valve overnight and when boat is left unattended
- Locate a fire blanket close to galley. The best way to smother fat flames and burning clothing
- Fit Galocarbon/CO2 fire extinguishers within easy reach of both ends of the galley.

Electrical

- Check for loose or corroded connections and broken strands, and replace
- Check that all circuits and retro fitted equipment like automatic bilge pumps, radios and starter motors are fused
- Install correct sized wiring rated to the input of the appliance.

Engine room

- Fit an auto extinguishing system in the engine room
- Keep the engine and bilges clean and check for oil leaks each time you go afloat
- Check fuel lines for leaks and damage from rubbing or vibration
- Store reserve fuel in a locker that drains outboard of the boat, and not into the bilge
- Don't keep oily rags onboard. Dispose of them after each trip.

Cabins

- Enforce a no-smoking policy below decks
- Fit a halocarbon/CO2 fire extinguisher in each cabin
- Check fire extinguishers every 6 months
- Turn them upside down and shake them
- Weigh them. If they fall below 0.25lb (0.11kg) of stated weight, replace them.

Outside elements

- Lightning can cause a serious fire, but not when you provide the charge with a continuous route to ground

- Connect the mast or steel radar/instrument bar to grounding plate on bottom of the hull or keel with No 4 AWG or heavy copper cable
- Do not connect it to the engine
- Charcoal can combust spontaneously when damp. If you must take charcoal aboard, seal it in plastic bags to keep it dry.

Fire fighting
- A fire requires air, fuel or heat. Remove one of these elements and the fire will extinguish itself
- Do not lift engine hatches
- Turn off fuel, gas and electricity

- Aim extinguishers at the base of the fire
- Splash water by hand rather than throw from a bucket
- Smother fat fires and clothing with a fire blanket
- Use the deck wash pump as a fire pump if necessary.

Abandon ship
- If the fire burns out of control, abandon ship
- Transmit Mayday
- Don life jackets
- Fire flares
- Launch liferaft.

This powerboat suffered a port engine fire. Quick action by her crew put the fire out and they were able to return to port unassisted.

Man overboard

This is every sailor's worst nightmare, and prevention is definitely better than cure. Being physically attached to the boat is an excellent first step, so clip on your lifelines if you have to go out on deck in heavy weather or at night. If you go overboard at night or in bad weather there is a significant risk that you will not be found, so practice man overboard drills regularly, and CLIP ON.

The fundamental components to the drill are:
- **STOP THE BOAT**
- **RAISE THE ALERT**
- **LOCATE THE CASUALTY**

If someone goes overboard, follow this standard procedure:
- Raise the alarm by shouting 'MAN OVERBOARD'.
- Keep at least one person looking and pointing at the casualty. This person is VITAL, and should not do anything else.
- Throw the danbuoy, horseshoe floats or large fender overboard immediately.
- Press the 'MOB' and then 'ENTER' buttons on the GPS.
- Start recovery manoeuvre (see following sections).
- In darkness use searchlight to illuminate search area.
- Send MAYDAY call on the VHF, satellite 'phone or DSC alert.

- Assume in temperate climate zones that the casualty will be suffering from hypothermia and prepare for this.

Recovery of Casualty
- Prepare a lasso to throw around the MOB
- Draw casualty towards bathing platform or lowest part of freeboard and attach boarding ladder or step fender.
- Grab casualty by the collar or lifejacket and pull them up onboard.

What to do if you are overboard
- DON'T PANIC. Panic will kill you long before the sea does.
- Inflate your lifejacket.
- Turn your light on by pulling the toggle.
- If you have a spray hood fitted into you lifejacket or oilskins, pull it down over your head if spray is making it difficult to breath.
- Locate the powerboat, but do not swim towards it

Practicing the man-overboard 'Williamson Turn'. One crewman should keep pointing at the victim throughout the procedure to give the helmsman a constant reference point.

- Locate any emergency equipment, e.g. the dan buoy, horseshoe or fender, thrown from the powerboat, and use it to aid flotation.
- Use your whistle to make sound signals, it is the best-value-for-money piece of lifesaving equipment you have. The sound is far easier to hear than shouting, and much less effort to produce.
- Do not expend energy - don't try to swim.
- Adopt the HELP (foetal) position.

Treatment against hypothermia
- Undress and change into warm clothes. Administer a warm non-alcoholic drink.
- Wrap in sleeping bag or blanket to re-warm slowly.
- Monitor and record symptoms at 15 minute intervals.
- Do not let casualty fall asleep.
- Call for assistance and get them checked out medically ashore.

Close quarter recovery

- Slow or stop and gauge wind direction.
- Turn bows and drive upwind
- Stop when wind is abeam of casualty.
- Drift downwind onto the MOB
- Use only the engine furthest away from MOB

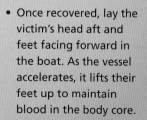

- Once recovered, lay the victim's head aft and feet facing forward in the boat. As the vessel accelerates, it lifts their feet up to maintain blood in the body core.

MOB

Williamson turn

- Recovery routine when travelling at speed or in strong conditions
- Note compass course and calculate reciprocal course
- Steer 60° to port or starboard to open up room to turn full circle and return down your own wake
- Turn helm hard over until boat is near to the reciprocal course then straighten up
- Follow boat's wake back, slow down and search for MOB
- Establish wind direction
- Once he/she is sighted, aim the boat a few metres to windward of casualty
- Stop and drift downwind onto the MOB, controlling the position of the boat with the engines
- Stop engines when making contact with the MOB.

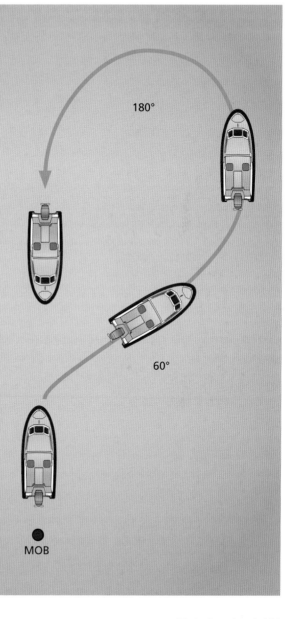

Glossary of terms

A

ABAFT – Behind or towards the stern.

ABEAM – At right angles to the boat.

AFT – See Abaft.

ALTO – Middle-level cloud base.

ALTOCUMULUS – Middle-level cloud.

ALTOSTRATUS – Middle-level cloud.

AMIDSHIPS – Centre of the boat.

ANCHOR – Device to moor the vessel in open water on the end of a line.

ANEMOMETER – Instrument to measure wind speed.

ANTICYCLONE – Meteorological term describing area of high pressure.

ANTIFOULING – Toxic paint to hinder weed and crustations from adhering to the hull

ATHWARTSHIPS – From one side of the vessel to the other.

B

BAILER – Scoop to remove water from inside the boat.

BALLAST – Additional weight carried in the hull to increase stability.

BEAM – Mid part of the boat, or measurement of maximum width of the hull.

BEAR AWAY – To turn the bows away from the wind.

BEARING – Compass direction.

BEAUFORT SCALE – Scale of wind speeds devised by Admiral Sir Francis Beaufort.

BECKET – A second eye or attachment point in a pulley block.

BIGHT – An open loop in a rope.

BLOCK – A pulley.

BLOCK AND TACKLE – A multi-purchase pulley system.

BOTTLE SCREW – Screw system used to tension rigging.

BOW – Front end of the boat.

BOLLARD – Vertical post on the quayside to make fast mooring lines.

BOWLINE – A knot used to tie a loop into the end of a rope.

BREAKWATER – Artificial wall around a harbour to break the force of the sea.

BROACH – When a boat slews out of control broadside to the wind and sea.

BULLSEYE – Wooden block or thimble with a hole drilled through it to take a rope to act as a block or stopper.

BULKHEAD – Transverse partition within the boat.

BUNG – Plug to block a drainage hole.

BUOY – Floating anchor, racing or navigation mark.

BUOYANCY – Power to float, having a density less than water.

BURGEE – Small flag flown from the masthead.

C

CAM CLEAT – Cleat with two spring-load cams to hold a rope.

CATAMARAN – Twin-hulled vessel.

CATHEDRAL HULL – Triple V-shaped hull

CAVITATION – Loss of propeller thrust caused by air bubbles forming on the blades.

CENTRE OF BUOYANCY – Point where the buoyant force of water acts on the hull.

CHART – Map of the sea.

CHINE – Line or crease in the hull. A hull built from flat sheets of plywood is known as a hard chine boat.

CIRRUS – High-level cloud.

CIRROCUMULUS – High-level cloud.

CIRROSTRATUS – High-level cloud with little form.

CLAM CLEAT – Cleat with no moving parts that secures rope within its grooved, V-shaped body.

CLEAR ASTERN / CLEAR AHEAD – One boat is clear astern of another when her hull and equipment in normal position are behind a line abeam from the after most point of the other boat's hull and equipment in normal position. The other boat is clear ahead.

CLEAT – Fitting designed to hold a rope under tension without the use of a knot or hitch.

CLEVIS PIN – Pin that closes the fork of a rigging screw.

CLINKER CONSTRUCTION – Traditional form of hull construction where the planks overlap each other.

CLOVE HITCH – Common knot or hitch used to tie a rope to a ring or rail.

COAMING – Small upstanding ledge or breakwater across or around the deck to deflect water.

COCKPIT – Open area of the vessel.

COMPASS – Navigation instrument that points to the magnetic north pole.

CUMULUS – Low-level cloud.

CUMULONIMBUS – Low-level rain cloud.

CURRENT – A stream of water.

D

DEAD RECKONING – Estimated position on a chart.

DEADRISE – Angle between bottom and chine or corner of hull.

DEEP-V HULL – See V Hull

DEPRESSION – Meteorological term for an area of low pressure.

DEVIATION – Compass error influenced by magnetic materials nearby.

DINGHY – Small open boat without a fixed keel.

DISPLACEMENT – Volume/weight that a hull displaces in water.

DODGER – Canvas folding hood erected to protect the cockpit from spray.

DORY – Open, stable sea going dinghy or tender.

DOWNWIND – travelling in the same direction as the wind.

DRAFT – The depth of water that a vessel draws

E

EASE – To slacken a rope.

EBB – Outgoing tide or flow.

ECHO SOUNDER – Sonar instrument that measures the depth of water.

EDDIES – Area of reverse or back-running current.

ENSIGN – national flag flown from a staff on the stern of a vessel.

F

FAIRLEAD – A fixed lead to guide a rope or sheet and prevent chafe.

FAIRWAY – Main navigable channel.

FATHOM – Nautical unit of measure equal to 6ft (2m).

FENDER – Portable cushion or inflatable bladder to protect the hull from rubbing against another boat or a pontoon.

FIGURE-OF-EIGHT KNOT – Stopper knot.

FIX – A vessel's position on a chart.

FLOOD TIDE – A rising tide.

FOLLOWING WIND – Opposite of headwind, when the wind comes from astern.

FOTHERING – The process of stuffing anything that comes to hand (e.g. sleeping bags) into a hole in the boat to stop water ingress.

FREEBOARD – Height of a boat's side above the water.

FRONT – Meteorological term describing a distinct line of weather – cold front, warm front, etc.

G

GEL COAT – The smooth waterproof outer resin coating of a fibre-reinforced moulded hull and deck.

GNOMONIC CHART – Navigation chart on which great circle arcs are projected as straight lines.

GO ABOUT – To tack through the eye of the wind.

GPS – Satellite-based global positioning system.

GRADIENT WIND – Meteorological term caused by changes in barometric pressure. The greater the change in pressure, the steeper the gradient.

GREENWICH MEAN TIME (GMT) – Now referred to as Universal Mean Time (UTC).

GRP – Glass reinforced plastic.

GUNWALE – Outer strengthening piece around the top of the hull.

H

HALF HITCH – Temporary knot to attach a rope to a rail.

HALYARD – Rope or wire line to hoist a flag or sails up the mast.

HARD CHINE – Line where the flat sheets used to construct a hull meet.

HEADING – Direction that a boat is taking.

HEAD TO WIND – Boat facing directly into wind.

HEAVE TO – To bring the boat to a halt.

HEAVING LINE – Light throwing line with a weight on the end to drag a heavier line across to another vessel or to shore.

HELM – Rudder. Also short for helmsman or helmsperson.

HELP POSITION – The heat escape lessening postion (foetal) position to adopt should you fall overboard.

HITCH – Type of knot for attaching a rope to a rail or hoop.

HOIST – Vertical dimension of a flag or sail.

HOVE TO – See Heave to.

HUMP SPEED – The speed at which hydrodynamic forces lift a planing hull up on top of the water, reducing drag and wave-making resistance.

I

IMMINENT – Meteorological term for change in weather within six hours.

INGLEFIELD CLIPS – Interlocking C-shaped clips used to attach signal flags.

INBOARD/OUTDRIVE – Inboard engine attached to a transom mounted steerable drive.

ISOBAR – Meteorological term for line on weather map linking points of equal atmospheric pressure.

J

JACKSTAY – A strong webbing strap running the length of the boat on each side. By clipping the lifeline to this, it ensures that 'Jack' stays on the boat.

JETTY – A structure extending out from harbour wall or beach on which to moor a vessel.

K

KEDGE – Light, temporary anchor to hold the boat against an adverse tidal stream.

KNOT – Nautical mile per hour (1 nautical mile equals 1.15 statute miles or 1,852m). Also refers to a rope tie.

KNUCKLE – Sharp longitudinal line of distortion within the hull.

L

LAND BREEZE – Offshore wind, opposite to a sea breeze, that develops when the temperature of the sea is higher than the land.

LANYARD – Short length of cord used as a safety line.

LATERAL RESISTANCE – Ability of a boat to resist leeway or sideways force of the wind.

LATITUDE– lines around the globe parallel to the Equator.

LEAD – The direction that a rope is led.

LEE – Opposite to windward. The side away from the wind.

LEE SHORE – Shoreline which the wind is blowing towards.

LEEWARD – Opposite of windward; away from the wind.

LIFEJACKET – Buoyancy vest designed to keep a nonswimmer or unconscious person floating head up.

LOA – Length overall.

LONGITUDE – Vertical line around the globe that passes through both north and south poles.

LWL – Load waterline or length of waterline.

M

MAGNETIC POLE – Point on the Earth's surface to which the needle of the compass points towards.

MAGNETIC VARIATION – Difference in angle between True North and Magnetic North.

MAMMA – Dark low-level rain cloud with udder-like shape.

MAST – A spar going straight up from the deck, used to attach sail and boom.

MARLING HITCH – Line of linked knots tying sail to a spar.

MERCATOR PROJECTION – Chart projection on which the lines of latitude and longitude are shown in parallel.

MERIDIAN – A line of longitude passing at right angles to lines of latitude.

MILLIBAR – Meteorological term for unit of pressure equal to 1/10000th of a bar.

MOULD – Male or female pattern for producing a plastic hull and other mouldings.

MULTIHULL – Generic term for a catamaran or trimaran.

MY – Prefix for name of vessel – Motor Yacht.

N

NAUTICAL ALMANAC – Annual publication listing tide tables, lights and radio beacons.

NAUTICAL MILE – 1 nautical mile equals 1.15 statute miles or 1,852m.

NEAP TIDES – Tides with the smallest rise and fall. Opposite of spring tides.

NIMBO – Rain cloud.

NIMBOSTRATUS – Middle-level rain cloud.

O

OAR – Wooden blade to row a boat with.

OBSTRUCTION – An object that a boat cannot pass without changing course substantially to avoid it, e.g. the shore, perceived underwater dangers or shallows.

OCCLUDED FRONT – Meteorological term to describe when a cold front overtakes a warm front.

OCCULTING LIGHT – Flashing navigation light where the period of light is longer than the period of darkness.

OFFSHORE WIND – Wind blowing seaward off the land.

OUTBOARD MOTOR – Self-contained propulsion system that bolts to the transom of a boat.

P

PAINTER – Mooring line.

PELICAN HOOK – Metal hook with a cam-action lock.

PFD – Personal flotation device such as a buoyancy aid or life jacket.

PINTLE – Male part of a pair of rudder hangings that fits into the female gudgeon.

PITCH – Theoretical distance that a propeller will move a vessel forward with one revolution.

PLANING – When a boat lifts its bows out of the water, and because of the reduced drag, then accelerates onto a planing attitude.

PORT – Left-hand side of a boat.

PULPIT – Safety guard rail around the bow.

PURCHASE – Mechanical advantage of the block and tackle or lever.

PUSHPIT – Safety guardrail around the stern.

Q

QUARTER – Sides of the boat aft, i.e. starboard quarter, port quarter.

R

RACE – Fast running tide or stream.

RADAR – **RA**dio **D**irection **A**nd **R**ange – Electronic navigation system that sends out radio pulses and transcribes their range and position on a cathode screen.

RADAR REFLECTOR – Metal or electrical system that magnifies the radio pulse from a radar scanner and reflects it back to the cathode screen.

REEF KNOT – Knot joining two ropes together.

RHUMB LINE – Line on the Earth's surface that intersects meridians at the same angle.

RIB – **R**igid bottomed **I**nflatable **B**oat.

RIDING LIGHT – Navigation light displayed at night by a vessel when lying at anchor.

RIDING TURN – When a rope or sheet crosses under itself and jams, most often around a winch.

RIGGING – Standing wires that hold up the mast.

RIGGING SCREW – Screw to tension shrouds. Also known as a bottle screw.

RIGHT OF WAY – Term within Collision Regulations denoting a boat with right of way.

ROCKER – Fore and aft curve within the central underside sections of the boat.

ROUND TURN AND TWO HALF HITCHES – Knot used to attach rope to a rail or hoop.

ROWLOCK – Swivel fitting on the gunwale to support an oar when rowing.

RUBBING STRAKE – A strengthening strip secured to the gunwale as a protective buffer.

RUDDER – Moving foil to steer the boat with.

S

SEA BREEZE – Onshore wind opposite to a land breeze, that develops when the temperature of the land is higher than the sea.

SELF BAILER – Thru-hull automatic bailer that, once activated, allows the bilge water to flow out when the boat is planing at speed.

SEACOCK – A valve going through the hull, which can be shut from inside the boat.

SEXTANT – A navigational instrument used to determine the vertical position of an object such as the Sun, Moon or stars. Used with celestial navigation.

SHACKLE – Metal link with screw pin to connect wires and lines.

SHEAVE – The wheel within a block.

SHEEPSHANK – Knot used to shorten a rope.

SHEET BEND – Knot used to join two dissimilar sized ropes together.

SHOCK CORD – Elastic or bungee cord made of rubber strands.

SKEG – Short keel to protect rudder from grounding.

SLIP LINE – Temporary double line with both ends made fast to the boat that can be released from onboard and pulled in.

SNAP SHACKLE – Shackle with a secure locking mechanism instead of a pin.

SPONSON – Inflatable tube around a RIB or inflatable dinghy.

SPRING TIDE – Extreme high tide caused by the gravitational pull of the moon.

STAND-ON-BOAT – Right of way boat.

STEPPED HULL – Right angle step in the bottom of a planing hull designed to suck air into the boundary layer and reduce skin friction.

SQUALL – Sudden, short-lived increase in wind.

STARBOARD – Right-hand side of the boat.

STEERAGE WAY – Enough speed for the rudder to steer the boat.

STEM – Forward extremity of the boat.

STERN – Aft extremity of the boat.

STRATUS – Featureless low-level cloud.

STRATOCUMULUS – Low-level cloud.

STROP – A ring of rope or wire used to make up an attachment to a spar.

SWIVEL – Connector whose two parts rotate.

SYNOPTIC CHART – Weather map.

T

TACKLE – Multi-purchase system.

TAIL – The free end of a rope.

TALURIT – Swaged wire splice.

THWART – Transverse seat or plank amidships.

TIDAL STREAM – Flow of water caused by the rise and fall of tide.

TIDE – Six-hourly rise and fall of water caused by the gravitational pull of the moon.

TILLER – Arm of a rudder to control boat direction.

TRANSIT – Sighting two objects in line.

TRANSOM – Transverse aft end of a boat.

TRIM TAB – Adjustable elevator to adjust the boat's fore and aft trim in the water.

TRUCKER'S HITCH – Knot used to tension a tie rope.

TRUE WIND – Direction and velocity of wind measured at a stationary position.

TUGMAN'S HITCH – Knot to secure towing strop to winch.

U

UNIVERSAL JOINT – Hinge that allows universal movement.

V

V HULL – Deep V hull has a deadrise of 18–25°.

VARIATION – Difference in angle between True North and Magnetic North.

VENTED HULL – See Stepped hull.

VMG – Velocity made good.

W

WAKE – Turbulence left astern of a moving boat.

WARP – Rope used to moor a boat.

WEATHER SHORE – Shoreline where the wind is blowing offshore.

WETTED SURFACE – Total underwater area of the hull.

WINCH – Capstan used to haul in an anchor cable.

WINDAGE – Drag caused by the boat and crew.

WINDWARD – Towards the wind; opposite of leeward.

WINDLASS – See Winch.

WORKING END – End of a rope used to tie a knot.

Acknowledgements

Our thanks to UKSA who have assisted with the production of this book, in particular, Jon Ely, Simon Rowell and Steve Rouse whose advice and contributions have been invaluable. They have answered questions, shaped the chapters and been a sounding board on many areas. A charity based in Cowes, UKSA is dedicated to changing lives through maritime activity, and trains almost 7,500 people every year from all backgrounds and to all levels. From children as young as 8 years old learning watersports skills, to the full range of RYA qualifications, and up to MCA Master 3000gt, UKSA is an expert in the watersports and yacht training industry. (*www.uksa.org*).

We must also thank designer Tony Castro for allowing the use of his Elan 35 and Galeon 440 power cruiser designs, Orkney Boats, builders of the Orkney range of sports fishing boats, and to Ribtec for the use of their Ribeye 6m RIB lines which all provide realism to the illustrations. A special thanks also goes to illustrator Greg Filip who worked so hard to faithfully reproduce the methodology taught by the UKSA.

David Houghton, the former weather guru to Britain's Olympic sailing team and author of *Weather at Sea* also provided valued advice.

Grateful thanks also go to Rowland Eno and the picture research team at PPL Photo Agency, for sourcing the many photographs we required to illustrate particular points throughout the book. We are also grateful to Force 4 Chandlery and Pains Wessex for the loan of safety equipment, to Spinlock for allowing us to use and demonstrate their Spinlock Deckvest and safety harness, and to Marlow Ropes for providing the cordage used in the chapter on knots and ropes.

Credits:
All illustrations: *Greg* Filip/PPL Photo Research: PPL *Photo Agency*. Photographs: Keith Pritchard 6, Barry Pickthall/PPL: 7, 8, 12, 22, 23, 27, 29, 32, 33, 34, 35, 36, 37, 38, 39, 40, 41, 44, 45, 50/1, 52, 53, 64, 67, 68, 71, 78, 82, 83, 129, 144, 162/3, 181. Mark Pepper/PPL: 9. Sally Collison: 10. Roy Roberts/PPL: 91. PPL 31, 36, 37, 38, 39, 92, 170. David Freeman: 92. Graham Franks: 93. Jon Nash: 94. Dave Porter/PPL: 94. Alberto Mariotti/PPL: 95. Nick Kirk/PPL: 96. Regulator Boats: 170. Icom UK Ltd: 160, 161. Orkney Boats: 6, 10, 83, 168. Tony Castro/Galeon Yachts: 7, 14, 48/49, 115. Volvo Penta: 25, 26, 64. Mercury: 24. Castoldi: 27. Ribtec Marine: 7, 13. Premier Marinas 28/28, 159. Tony Castro/ Elan: 10, 51. UKSA: 10, 43, 57, 85, 93, 112, 137, 141, 143, 164/165. Intrepid Powerboats: 11. Glacier Bay Catamarans: 11, Edgewater Boats: 15, Neil Grundy/PPL: 36, 37, 38, 39, 41. Glastron Boats: 46/47, 88/89. Chris*Craft: 84. On Edition: 29, RNLI: 172. James Walker/PPL: 177.

ENJOYABLE TRAINING & QUALIFICATIONS

Free guidance and advice
Just call 0800 781 1080

RYA Training Centre

Visit www.uksa.org

Registered charity number: 299248

UKSA